CCSS Prep
Grade 7
Editing and Revising

by Sarah M. W. Espano and Dana Konopka
Edited by Patricia F. Braccio

Item Code RAS 2715 • Copyright © 2013 Queue, Inc.

Queue, Inc. • 80 Hathaway Drive, Stratford, CT 06615
(800) 232-2224 • Fax: (800) 775-2729 • www.qworkbooks.com

TABLE OF CONTENTS

TO THE STUDENTS

In this editing and revising workbook, you will read many passages. You will then answer multiple-choice questions about what you have read.

As you read and answer the questions, please remember:

- You may refer back to the passage as often as you like.

- Read each question very carefully and choose the **best** answer.

- Indicate the correct multiple-choice answers directly in this workbook. Circle or underline the correct answer.

- Remember what you know about correct grammar, punctuation, and English usage.

Justin is in the seventh grade. His teacher asked each student to choose a myth that he or she liked and to summarize the story. Justin chose a Mexican myth. First, he made an outline of his ideas. Then he wrote his rough draft. Now he needs your help editing and revising it.

Here is Justin's rough draft. Read it and then answer questions 1–10.

(1) The myth of the "Twin Brothers" is a famous Mexican myth that tells how the sun and the moon came to be. (2) It is the story of two brothers who were the grandsons of the Father and Mother gods. (3) The grandparents had helped Hurakan the god of lightning, to create the earth.

(4) Long ago there were two brother gods who were very good at playing a ball game called "tlachtli." (5) One day they make the mistake of playing very close to the edge of Hades. (6) The two kings that ruled Hades sent owl messengers to invite the two brothers to a game of tlachtli. (7) "Great! (8) Now we can defeat our enemies," said the brave brothers.

(9) When the brothers got to Hades, they were killed. (10) One of the brothers had fallen in love with a princess of Hades and had secretly married her before his death. (11) One of the kings found out about this and drove her out of the kingdom. (12) She came to the earth and found the mother of her murdered husband. (13) She bore twin sons and they lived together with their grandmother and their two half-brothers.

(14) The twin sons were named Hun-Apu and Xbalanque. (15) Their half-brothers did not like Hun-Apu and Xbalanque, the worst-behaved little boys in the world. (16) When the half-brothers teased the twins, Hun-Apu and Xbalanque turned them into something else. (17) When their grandmother gave them work to do in the fields and they didn't do any of it. (18) They cast a spell on the farm tools. (19) The tools did all the work by themselves.

(20) One day a rat told the twins the story about how their father and uncle had died in Hades. (21) The twins were determined to avenge their deaths. (22) They went straight to their grandmother and asked for the clubs and balls so they could go play tlachtli in Hades. (23) She gave them the clubs and balls, and off they went to Hades.

(24) The rat had told Hun-Apu and Xbalanque about the tricks that the kings of Hades had played on their father and uncle. (25) The twins were ready for anything. (26) They didn't fall for any of the kings' tricks and they won the game of tlachtli. (27) The kings got mad and tried to kill them. (28) Then they realized that Hun-Apu and Xbalanque were immortal they could not be killed. (29) The foolish kings tried to prove that they were immortal, too. (30) They said, "let us be killed, so that we can see what it's like to come back to life, too." (31) Then Hun-Apu and Xbalanque killed the kings, and they never came back to life again.

(32) The twins rescued the souls of their father and uncle and sent them into the heavens. (33) The father and uncle became the sun and the moon. (34) They are still shining in our skies today.

1. Choose the correct way to write the underlined part of sentence 3.

   The grandparents had helped <u>Hurakan the god of lightning,</u> to create the earth.

   a. Hurakan the god of lightening,
   b. Hurakan, the god of lightning,
   c. Hurakan the god, of lightning,
   d. No change is needed.

2. Read sentence 28, which is poorly written.

   Then they realized that Hun-Apu and Xbalanque were immortal they could not be killed.

   Choose the **best** way to rewrite this sentence.

   a. Then they realized that Hun-Apu and Xbalanque were immortal and could not be killed.
   b. Then they realized that Hun-Apu and Xbalanque because they were immortal they could not be killed.
   c. Then they, realizing that Hun-Apu and Xbalanque were immortal, could not be killed.
   d. Then they realized that Hun-Apu and Xbalanque were immortal could not be killed.

3. Choose the correct way to write the underlined part of sentence 30.

   <u>They said, "let us be killed,</u> so that we can see what it's like to come back to life, too."

   a. They said ", let us be killed,
   b. They said "let us be killed,
   c. They said, "Let us be killed,
   d. No change is needed.

4. Choose the correct way to write sentence 5.

   One day they <u>make the mistake of playing very close to the edge of Hades.</u>

   a. make the mistake of playing very close to the edge of Hades?
   b. make the mistake of playing very close to the edge of hades.
   c. made the mistake of playing very close to the edge of Hades.
   d. No change is needed.

5. Which of these is **not** a complete sentence?

   a. The two kings that ruled Hades sent owl messengers to invite the two brothers to a game of tlachtli.
   b. When their grandmother gave them work to do in the fields and they didn't do any of it.
   c. The foolish kings tried to prove that they were immortal, too.
   d. The twins rescued the souls of their father and uncle and sent them into the heavens.

6. Choose the **best** way to combine the ideas in sentences 18 and 19 into one sentence.

   They cast a spell on the farm tools. The tools did all the work by themselves.

   a. Doing all the work by themselves, they cast a spell on the farm tools.
   b. They cast a spell on the farm tools the tools did all the work by themselves.
   c. They cast a spell on the farm tools and who did all the work by themselves.
   d. They cast a spell on the farm tools, and the tools did all the work by themselves.

7. Justin wants to change sentence 16 so that it is more specific.

   When the half-brothers teased the twins, Hun-Apu and Xbalanque turned them <u>into something else.</u>

   Choose the **best** way to rewrite the underlined part of this sentence.

   a. into different animals.
   b. to be different from what they were before.
   c. into a couple of silly-looking apes.
   d. to make them look silly.

8. Justin wants to add this sentence to the paragraph that begins with sentence 20.

    The grandmother was reluctant, but she knew the boys had a job to do.

    Where would the sentence **best** fit?

    a. right after sentence 20
    b. right after sentence 21
    c. right after sentence 22
    d. right after sentence 23

9. Choose the correct way to write the underlined part of sentence 26.

    They <u>didn't fall for any of the kings' tricks</u> and they won the game of tlachtli.

    a. didn't fall for any of the kings tricks
    b. didn't fell for any of the kings' tricks
    c. didn't fall for any of the king's tricks
    d. No change is needed.

10. Choose the word or phrase that **best** fits at the beginning of sentence 15.

    a. First,
    b. Unfortunately,
    c. For example,
    d. Moreover,

4

Kenita is in the seventh grade. The Board of Education is considering making the school day longer by one hour each day. Kenita's teacher asked each student to write a letter to the school superintendent to persuade her to accept or reject this idea. Kenita organized her ideas and wrote her rough draft. Now she needs your help editing and revising it.

Here is Kenita's rough draft. Read it and then answer questions 1–10.

(1) dear Dr. Frenette,

(2) I know that you have reasons for wanting to make the school day one hour longer. (3) A longer school day would allow students more time to learn. (4) Teachers would have more time to help students who need extra help. (5) Students could do enrichment projects who were done with their work. (6) A longer school day would help working parents because their children will be safe at school in the afternoon.

(7) I still think that making the school day one hour longer is not the best idea. (8) Us kids are not like grownups who can work a long day. (9) By three o'clock in the afternoon, most kids are already pretty tired from all that school work. (10) Before tackling our homework we need to go rest our brains.

(11) When I need extra help with my work, I bring it to Mrs. Pow, and she always helps me figure it out. (12) Sometimes I learn from my classmates, to. (13) However, I learn best when I focus on the task and work by myself. (14) I can do that at home or in the after-school program, and I don't need an extra hour of classes to learn more. (15) Sometimes I think it's better we having to do things by ourselves. (16) It makes us more independent.

(17) If you are worried about the safety of students who's parents work, I think you should make the after-school program available to everyone for free. (18) Then the students would be safe and the parents would have peace of mind the kids would be able to play or get their homework done. (19) I like the relaxed atmosphere in the after-school program. (20) Maybe there could be special classes once in a while that the students could choose to take. (21) I would like to learn photography.

(22) I hope that you will agree that improving the after-school program would be better than making the school day one hour longer. (23) Thank you for considering my opinion.

(24) Sincerely,

(25) Kenita Williams

1. Choose the correct way to write the underlined part of sentence 8.

   <u>Us kids are not like grownups</u> who can work a long day.

   a. We kids are not like grownups
   b. Us kid's are not like grownups
   c. Us kids is not like grownups
   d. No change is needed.

2. Choose the correct way to write the underlined part of sentence 10.

   <u>Before tackling our homework we need</u> to go rest our brains.

   a. Before our tackling homework we need
   b. Before tackled our homework we need
   c. Before tackling our homework, we need
   d. No change is needed.

3. Choose the correct way to write the underlined part of sentence 17.

   If you are worried about the <u>safety of students who's parents work,</u> I think you should make the after-school program available to everyone for free.

   a. safety of student's who's parents work,
   b. safety of students whose parents work,
   c. safty of students who's parents work,
   d. No change is needed.

6

4. Read sentence 18, which is poorly written.

   Then the students would be safe and the parents would have peace of mind the kids would be able to play or get their homework done.

   Choose the **best** way to rewrite this sentence.

   a. Then the students would be safe, the parents would have peace of mind, and the kids would be able to play or get their homework done.
   b. Then the students would be safe and the parents would have peace of mind and the kids would be able to play or get their homework done.
   c. Then the students would be safe. And the parents would have peace of mind and the kids would be able to play or get their homework done.
   d. Then the students would be safe. The parents would have peace of mind. The kids would be able to play. Or they could get their homework done.

5. The topic sentence of the paragraph that begins with sentence 2 is

   a. sentence 2.
   b. sentence 4.
   c. sentence 5.
   d. sentence 6.

6. Choose the correct way to write line 1, the opening of the letter.

   dear Dr. Frenette,

   a. dear dr. Frenette,
   b. dear Dr. Frenette?
   c. Dear Dr. Frenette,
   d. No change is needed.

7. Choose the correct way to write the underlined part of sentence 12.

   Sometimes I <u>learn from my classmates, to.</u>

   a. learn from my clasmates, to.
   b. learn from my classmates, too.
   c. learn from his classmates, to.
   d. No change is needed.

8. Read sentence 5, which is poorly written.

Students could do enrichment projects who were done with their work.

Choose the **best** way to rewrite this sentence.

   a. Students could do enrichment projects that were done with their work.
   b. Students who were done with their work could do enrichment projects.
   c. Students could do enrichment projects being done with their work.
   d. Who were done with their work, students could do enrichment projects.

9. Read sentence 15, which is poorly written.

Sometimes I think it's better we having to do things by ourselves.

Choose the **best** way to rewrite this sentence.

   a. Sometimes I think having better things to do by ourselves.
   b. Sometimes I think it's better we are, to do things by ourselves.
   c. Sometimes I think it's better we were having to do things by ourselves.
   d. Sometimes I think it's better when we have to do things by ourselves.

10. Choose the correct way to write the underlined part of sentence 6.

A longer school day would help working parents because <u>their children will be safe</u> at school in the afternoon.

   a. their children would be safe
   b. they're children will be safe
   c. their childs will be safe
   d. No change is needed.

Brian's seventh-grade teacher asked each student to write a report about ocean microbes and the role that they play in our world. Brian took notes at the library, organized his thoughts, and wrote his rough draft. Now he needs your help editing and revising it.

Here is Brian's rough draft. Read it and then answer questions 1–10.

(1) Every drop of ocean water is alive with tiny sea creatures called "microbes." (2) A microbe is a living organism that is too small to be seen without a microscope. (3) Most of these microbes are one-celled organisms called "bacteria." (4) Maybe these little creatures don't seem very significant, but they are if it weren't for them, life as we know it could not exist.

(5) Ocean bacteria are the most commonest creatures on the planet. (6) There are billions of them in just one teaspoon of sea water. (7) Even though the microbes are so tiny, scientists believe that if we put them all together, they would weigh as much as all the fish in the oceans combind.

(8) Ocean bacteria has some very important jobs to do. (9) Some bacteria live close to the surface where they get a lot of sunlight. (10) These bacteria carry out photosynthesis. (11) They produce about one-half of all the oxygen that we breathe. (12) Some bacteria live in the deeper waters instead. (13) It's hard to believe that there could be life in such a deep, dark place. (14) These cool bacteria have evolved to get their energy from chemicals instead of the sun. (15) They are responsible for decomposing dead material that falls to the bottom of the ocean. (16) Ocean bacteria affect the amount of carbon that is present in the ocean. (17) Carbon is an element that is necessary for all living things. (18) The amount of carbon in the ocean affects how much carbon dioxide there is in the earth's atmosphere.

(19) Living in the deepest ocean rocks, scientists recently discovered bacteria. (20) They eat chemicals and can live without any light in almost boiling hot water. (21) They get their energy from the minerals in the rocks. (22) Some scientists believe that these bacteria could exist beneath the surface of Mars.

(23) Imagine the world without ocean bacteria. (24) The sea would be full of dead creatures, and the land creatures would not have enough oxygen to breathe. (25) There might been enough carbon dioxide in our atmosphere to raise temperatures all over the world. (26) Ocean microbes are a extremely important part of life on Earth.

1. Choose the correct way to write the underlined part of sentence 25.

   There might been enough carbon dioxide in our atmosphere to raise temperatures all over the world.

   a. There might been enough carbon dioxide in her
   b. There might been enough carbon dioxide, in our
   c. There might be enough carbon dioxide in our
   d. No change is needed.

2. Read sentence 4, which is poorly written.

   Maybe these little creatures don't seem very significant, but they are if it weren't for them, life as we know it could not exist.

   Choose the **best** way to rewrite this sentence.

   a. Maybe these little creatures don't seem very significant, but they are, and if it weren't for them, life as we know it, could not exist.
   b. Maybe these little creatures don't seem very significant, but they are. If it weren't for them, life as we know it could not exist.
   c. Maybe these little creatures don't seem very significant. But they are if it weren't for them, life as we know it could not exist.
   d. Maybe these little creatures don't seem very significant. But they are if it weren't for them. Life as we know it could not exist.

3. Choose the correct way to write the underlined part of sentence 7.

   Even though the microbes are so tiny, scientists believe that if we put them all together, they would weigh as <u>much as all the fish in the oceans combind.</u>

   a. much as all the fish in the oceans combined.
   b. much as all the fish in the ocean's combind.
   c. much of all the fish in the oceans combind.
   d. No change is needed.

4. Choose the correct way to write the underlined part of sentence 8.

Ocean <u>bacteria has some very important</u> jobs to do.

   a. bacterias has some very important
   b. bacteria have some very important
   c. bacteria has some very, important
   d. No change is needed.

5. Choose the sentence that could **best** be added right after sentence 18.

   a. Ocean microbes are some of the tiniest known living things.
   b. Can you imagine what would happen if there was an underwater earthquake?
   c. Earth's atmosphere is denser than that of Mars.
   d. Carbon dioxide is a gas that contributes to global warming.

6. Choose the word or phrase that **best** fits at the beginning of sentence 14.

   a. However,
   b. Unfortunately,
   c. In addition,
   d. Moreover,

7. Choose the correct way to write the underlined part of sentence 5.

Ocean bacteria are <u>the most commonest creatures</u> on the planet.

   a. the most commoner creatures
   b. the most common creatures
   c. the most commonest creature's
   d. No change is needed.

8. Brian wants to change sentence 14 so that it is more specific.

    These <u>cool</u> bacteria have evolved to get their energy from chemicals instead of the sun.

    Choose the **best** way to rewrite the underlined part of this sentence.

    a. neat
    b. good
    c. hardy
    d. interesting

9. Read sentence 19, which is poorly written.

    Living in the deepest ocean rocks, scientists recently discovered bacteria.

    Choose the **best** way to rewrite this sentence.

    a. Living in the deepest ocean rocks that the scientists recently discovered bacteria.
    b. Scientists, living in the deepest ocean rocks, recently discovered bacteria.
    c. Scientists recently discovered bacteria living in the deepest ocean rocks.
    d. In the deepest ocean rocks living, scientists recently discovered bacteria.

10. Choose the correct way to write the underlined part of sentence 26.

    Ocean microbes are <u>a extremely important part of life</u> on Earth.

    a. an extremely important part of life
    b. a extremely important parts of life
    c. a extremely, important part of life
    d. No change is needed.

Shelby's seventh-grade class is learning about different forms of government. Her teacher asked each student to reflect on all that the class had learned and to write an essay describing his or her own personal definition of a democracy. Shelby made an outline of her ideas and then wrote her rough draft. Now she needs your help editing and revising it.

Here is Shelby's rough draft. Read it and then answer questions 1–10.

(1) What is a democracy? (2) This is a very tough question. (3) I think that each person would have a slightly different definition of a democracy.

(4) To me, the word, "democracy," means "fairness." (5) A democracy is a system of government that tries to be fair to each and every person. (6) In a democracy, there's no dictators and no ruling classes. (7) In a democracy, the people vote to elect their leaders, and the leaders serve the people. (8) In a democracy, everyone can participate in the government. (9) There is no discrimination against anyone because of his or her race, gender, or religion. (10) People are free to speak their minds against the government without having to be afraid of punishment. (11) In a democracy, people can live the way they want to live without the government telling them where they have to live, what they have to wear, or what they have to believe.

(12) In a democracy, everyone should be able to live the way he or she wants to live. (13) However, it's not as simple as it sounds. (14) Suppose you are a scientist and you want to experiment with some deadly viruses in your home laboratory. (15) Then the government finds out what you are doing. (16) The government forces you to give up your research. (17) You might say "That's not fair!" (18) It isn't fair to your community, though, when you put people's lives in jeopardy. (19) In a democracy, an individual's rights are honored only as long as they are not a threat other people. (20) To be fair, a democracy has to have some limits.

(21) Governments are not the only things that can be called democracies. (22) A dictator is a person who has absolute power over the people in his or her country. (23) A home could be a democracy. (24) If all the members of a family work together to make the house rules, then their home is a democracy.

(25) People who live in a democracy have some important responsibilities. (26) Vote, learn what's going on, and speak up for what you believe. (27) Otherwise, nothing will ever change for the better. (28) We americans are fortunate to live in a democratic society. (29) Paying attention to our country and making it an even better place someday.

1. The topic sentence of the paragraph that begins with sentence 12 is

    a. sentence 12.
    b. sentence 16.
    c. sentence 18.
    d. sentence 20.

2. Choose the correct way to write the underlined part of sentence 17.

    You might <u>say "That's not fair!"</u>

    a. say, "That's not fair!"
    b. say "That's not fair?"
    c. say "Thats not fair!"
    d. No change is needed.

3. The paragraph that begins with sentence 4 is poorly written. Choose the **best** way to rewrite sentence 8 so that the paragraph does not repeat ideas.

    In a democracy, everyone can participate in the government.

    a. In a democracy, it's where everyone can participate in the government.
    b. Everyone can participate in a democratic government.
    c. In a democracy, everyone in the government can participate.
    d. Everyone in a democracy can participate in the government.

4. Choose the sentence that could **best** be added right after sentence 24.

    a. The president is the elected leader of our country.
    b. I am glad that the United States is a democratic country.
    c. India is called "the largest democracy in the world," but its government is very different from our government.
    d. At school, too, our classroom is a democracy when we vote.

5. Choose the sentence that does **not** belong in the paragraph that begins with sentence 21.

   a. sentence 21
   b. sentence 22
   c. sentence 23
   d. sentence 24

6. Choose the correct way to write the underlined part of sentence 28.

   <u>We americans are fortunate</u> to live in a democratic society.

   a. We americans is fortunate
   b. We Americans are fortunate
   c. We american's are fortunate
   d. No change is needed.

7. Choose the **best** way to combine the ideas in sentences 15 and 16 into one sentence.

   Then the government finds out what you are doing. The government forces you to give up your research.

   a. Then the government finds out what you are doing because the government forces you to give up your research.
   b. Then the government finds out what you are doing, the government forces you to give up your research.
   c. Then the government finds out what you are doing and forces you to give up your research.
   d. Then the government finds out what you are doing but the government forced you to give up your research.

15

8. Which of these is **not** a complete sentence?

   a. In a democracy, people can live the way they want to live without the government telling them where they have to live, what they have to wear, or what they have to believe.
   b. Suppose you are a scientist and you want to experiment with some deadly viruses in your home laboratory.
   c. If all the members of a family work together to make the house rules, then their home is a democracy.
   d. Paying attention to our country and making it an even better place someday.

9. Choose the correct way to write the underlined part of sentence 6.

   In a democracy, <u>there's no dictators and</u> no ruling classes.

   a. there's no dictator's and
   b. there are no dictators and
   c. there's no dictators, and
   d. No change is needed.

10. Choose the correct way to write the underlined part of sentence 24.

    If all the members of a family work together to make the house rules, <u>then their home is a democracy.</u>

    a. than their home is a democracy.
    b. then their homes is a democracy.
    c. then they're home is a democracy.
    d. No change is needed.

Joel is in the seventh grade. His teacher asked each student to think about what would happen if the taxes were raised on fast food. Each student then had to decide whether or not he or she supported the tax hike and to explain why or why not. Joel organized his thoughts and wrote the rough draft of a persuasive essay. Now he needs your help editing and revising it.

Here is Joel's rough draft. Read it and then answer questions 1–10.

(1) Everybody knows that eating too much fast food is bad for your health. (2) Some people think that if we raised the taxes on fast food, people would eat less of it and be healthier. (3) Sure, we could use the extra tax money to spend on education or health care. (4) I do not agree that raising taxes on fast food is a good idea.

(5) I think that raising taxes on fast food is unfair to the restaurants. (6) This is a country of equal oportunity, and it doesn't seem right to me that the government would make it harder for certain restaurants to sell their food. (7) It isn't like the restaurants are selling cigarettes. (8) Cigarettes have been proven to cause cancer. (9) Fast food may be bad for you, but most people do not eat them every day. (10) In addition, most fast food restaurants today also sell some healthy food. (11) How would we ever decide which foods get taxed and which ones didn't? (12) I would not like to be the store manager who has to keep track of all the different tax rates for the items on the menu.

(13) Raising taxes are also unfair to the customers. (14) What we eat is a personal choice. (15) I think it would be unfair for the government to charge extra tax for certain foods that people choose to eat. (16) Then it would no longer be a truly free choice. (17) When you go into a fast food restaurant you always see families with kids eating there. (18) They want a quick and easy meal that everyone likes, and they don't want to pay a lot for it. (19) A tax on fast food, more difficult for families to eat out.

(20) There is another problem with taxing fast food. (21) Restaurants are not the only place where we can buy fast food. (22) Grocery stores sell it, too. (23) Who decides which grocery store items get taxed and which ones don't? (24) We would need a federal bureau with fast food patrol units all over the country. (25) My father is a police officer. (26) It doesn't seem very practical to me.

(27) Fast food is not the healthiest kind of food in the world, but it does not deserve the punishment of added taxes. (28) There are better ways to raise money for health and education. (29) Let's get real and tax all food equally.

1. Choose the correct way to write the underlined part of sentence 17.

   When you go <u>into a fast food restaurant you always see families</u> with kids eating there.

   a. into a fast food restaurant. You always see families
   b. into a fast food restaurant, you always see families
   c. into a fast food restaurant and always see families
   d. No change is needed.

2. Choose the word or phrase that **best** fits at the beginning of sentence 4.

   a. For example,
   b. In addition,
   c. However,
   d. Fortunately,

3. Choose the correct way to write the underlined part of sentence 13.

   Raising taxes <u>are also unfair to the customers.</u>

   a. are also unfair too the customers.
   b. are also unfair to the custemers.
   c. is also unfair to the customers.
   d. No change is needed.

4. Which of these is **not** a complete sentence?

   a. I think that raising taxes on fast food is unfair to the restaurants.
   b. Fast food may be bad for you, but most people do not eat them every day.
   c. A tax on fast food, more difficult for families to eat out.
   d. It doesn't seem very practical to me.

5. Choose the **best** way to combine the ideas in sentences 7 and 8 into one sentence.

   It isn't like the restaurants are selling cigarettes. Cigarettes have been proven to cause cancer.

   a. It isn't like the restaurants are selling cigarettes have been proven to cause cancer.
   b. It isn't like the restaurants are selling cigarettes, but cigarettes are cancerous.
   c. Proven to cause cancer, the restaurants are not selling cigarettes.
   d. It isn't like the restaurants are selling cigarettes, which have been proven to cause cancer.

6. Choose the correct way to write the underlined part of sentence 9.

   Fast food may be bad for you, but <u>most people do not eat them</u> every day.

   a. most people do not eat it
   b. mostest people do not eat them
   c. most people does not eat them
   d. No change is needed.

7. Choose the correct way to write the underlined part of sentence 11.

   How would we ever decide which foods get taxed and <u>which ones didn't?</u>

   a. which ones didn't!
   b. which, ones didn't?
   c. which ones don't?
   d. No change is needed.

8. Choose the sentence that does **not** belong in the paragraph that begins with sentence 20.

   a. sentence 21
   b. sentence 23
   c. sentence 24
   d. sentence 25

9. Choose the **best** way to write the underlined part of sentence 29 so that the composition maintains a consistent tone.

   <u>Let's get real and</u> tax all food equally.

   a. Let's get a grip and
   b. Come on, let's just
   c. Let's be fair and
   d. Don't be ridiculous. Let's

10. Choose the correct way to write the underlined part of sentence 6.

   <u>This is a country of equal oportunity,</u> and it doesn't seem right to me that the government would make it harder for certain restaurants to sell their food.

   a. This is a country of equal oportunity,
   b. This are a country of equal oportunity,
   c. This is a country of equals oportunity,
   d. No change is needed.

Heidi's seventh-grade French class has been studying French painters and sculptors. Her teacher requests that each student write a report on an artist of his or her choosing. Heidi loves Henri Matisse's work and decides to write her report about him. After researching and writing her first draft, she needs some help revising it.

Here is Heidi's rough draft. Read it and then answer questions 1–10.

(1) Henri Matisse was one of the most famous French artists of all time. (2) He was an accomplished sculptor, painter, and graphic designer. (3) As leader of a movement called "Fauvism," Matisse left a bold mark on art as we know it today.

(4) Henri Matisse was born on December 31, 1869, in Le Cateau in France. (5) He have been described as a slow, methodical leader who taught and encouraged other painters. (6) Some biographers say he was an anxious man, who eased his nervousness by painting. (7) Matisse himself described his art as "a good armchair." (8) Another way of saying that it was a comfort to him.

(9) Matisse first began painting while recovering from an operation. (10) He moved to Paris in 1891 to study art. (11) Less than a decade after moving to Paris, Matisse was leading a group of artists called the "Fauvists." (12) Fauvism flourished in France from 1898 to 1908. (13) These artists used pure, brilliant color—often straight from the tube—to create what has been described as "an explosion on the canvas." (14) Matisse believed that the arrangement of color in a piece of art was as important in communicating meaning as the painting's subject matter. (15) He chose to paint bright colors and strong lines over detail, a style that greatly differed from the Impressionist painters of the late nineteenth and early twentieth centuries. (16) Fauvists did like the Impressionists did and painted directly from nature, but the works they did were more expressive and less traditional.

(17) In 1905, Matisse and other Fauvists exhibited their paintings at the Salon d'Automne for the first time. (18) The bright colors and bold forms shocked the Paris art world. (19) Matisse exbihited his famous *Woman with the Hat*. (20) This painting has brisk strokes of blue, green, and red. (21) The colors and strokes form an energetic, expressive view of a woman. (22) A critic of the time Louis Vauxcelles called the painters "Les Fauves," which translates to "Wild Beasts." (23) He found their work to be too violent.

(24) In 1941, following a rich artistic career, Matisse was diagnosed with duodenal cancer. (25) He was confined to a wheelchair. (26) But anyway, he didn't stop working as an artist. (27) When he was too weak to stand at his easel, he began papercuts, or colored-paper collages. (28) The 1950 piece *Beasts of the Sea* gives you the feeling that you are underwater among fish, sea horses, and coral.

(29) Henri Matisse died on November 3, 1954, in Nice in France. (30) His artistic path was long and varied, covering many different styles along the way. (31) Overall, we see that he was one of the finest, most influential artists of our time.

1. The paragraph that begins with sentence 9 is poorly written. Choose the **best** way to rewrite sentence 11 so that the paragraph does not repeat ideas.

   Less than a decade after moving to Paris, Matisse was leading a group of artists called "Fauvists."

   a. Less than a decade after Matisse was leading a group of artists called "Fauvists," he had already moved to Paris.
   b. Less than a decade later, Matisse was leading a group of artists called "Fauvists."
   c. A group of artists called "Fauvists" led Matisse less than a decade after he moved to Paris.
   d. A decade after Matisse moved to Paris, the "Fauvists" were being led by Matisse.

2. Which of these is **not** a complete sentence?

   a. Fauvists did like the Impressionists did and painted directly from nature, but the works they did were more expressive and less traditional.
   b. He found their work to be too violent.
   c. Another way of saying that it was a comfort to him.
   d. Henri Matisse died on November 3, 1954, in Nice in France.

3. Choose the correct way to write the underlined part of sentence 22.

   <u>A critic of the time Louis Vauxcelles called</u> the painters "Les Fauves," which translates to "Wild Beasts."

   a. A critic of the time, Louis Vauxcelles, called
   b. A critic, of the time, Louis Vauxcelles called
   c. A critic of the times Louis Vauxcelles called
   d. No change is needed.

4. Choose the correct way to write the underlined part of sentence 19.

    Matisse exbihited his famous *Woman with the Hat.*

    a. Matisse exbihited his famuos
    b. Matisse exhibited his famous
    c. Matisse exbihited his' famous
    d. No change is needed.

5. Choose the **best** way to write the underlined part of sentence 26 so that the composition maintains a consistent tone.

    But anyway, he didn't stop working as an artist.

    a. Still, he continued
    b. Nothing could stop him cuz he just wanted to be
    c. It was really special for him to be
    d. He could because he wanted to keep

6. Choose the **best** way to combine the ideas in sentences 20 and 21 into one sentence.

    This painting has brisk strokes of blue, green, and red. The colors and strokes form an energetic, expressive view of a woman.

    a. This painting of an energetic, expressive woman is done in brisk strokes of blue, green, and red.
    b. Blue, green, and red form an energetic, expressive view of a woman in the painting.
    c. This painting forms an energetic, expressive woman's view of blue, green, and red.
    d. This painting has brisk strokes of blue, green, and red that form an energetic, expressive view of a woman.

7. The topic sentence of the paragraph that begins with sentence 17 is

    a. sentence 17.
    b. sentence 20.
    c. sentence 22.
    d. sentence 23.

8. Choose the correct way to write the underlined part of sentence 30.

His artistic <u>path was long and varied,</u> covering many different styles along the way.

   a. path was long, and varied,
   b. path was long and vareed,
   c. path were long and varied,
   d. No change is needed.

9. Choose the correct way to write the underlined part of sentence 5.

<u>He have been described as a slow, methodical leader</u> who taught and encouraged other painters.

   a. He have been described as a slow, methodicical leader
   b. He has been described as a slow, methodical leader
   c. He have been described as a slow. Methodical leader
   d. No change is needed.

10. Read sentence 16, which is poorly written.

Fauvists did like the Impressionists did and painted directly from nature, but the works they did were more expressive and less traditional.

Choose the **best** way to rewrite this sentence.

   a. Fauvists painted directly from nature as the Impressionists had before them, but their works were more expressive and less traditional.
   b. Impressionists painted directly from nature and so did the Fauvists, and their works were more expressive and less traditional.
   c. Fauvists and Impressionists both painted from nature, but the Fauvists did works that were more expressive and they did works that were less traditional.
   d. Impressionists and Fauvists, directly from nature they painted, but their works were more expressive and less traditional.

Drew has been learning about dialogue and creative writing in his seventh-grade English class. The teacher told the students that they must write a creative story with dialogue. Drew brainstormed some ideas and made a web of elements he wanted to include. He wrote his first draft and needs help editing and revising part of it.

Here is Drew's rough draft. Read it and then answer questions 1–10.

(1) "I can't take it!" (2) The man clenched his meaty hands against his temples and locked his jaw. (3) "The stress will kill me, I swear it!" (4) His massive shoulders seemed to swell out from under a undersized overcoat, a relic of a time when men wore suits no matter what their employ. (5) "Could it be that I don't write as good as I think I do?"

(6) "Impossible, Evan," replied a frail man who seemed made of the most thinner crepe. (7) His iridescent skin revealed his slight bone structure. (8) His hollowed eyes hung loosely in they're sockets, and his cheekbones were sharp points jutting out from a concave face. (9) "This is what you were destined to become. (10) You were meant to be the world's most famous author and you will be! (11) I would bet my life on it."

(12) Evan Driscoll drove his pen into the tabletop. (13) "I've had enough of your groveling," he snarled. (14) "You will be a world-famous editor the moment I become a world-famous author and no sooner. (15) You'll get no scraps from me by trying to lick my boot heels like a common peasant."

(16) Driscoll's monstrous frame shuddered and heaved as he tried to summon the strength to continue. (17) His assistant, the sniveling Mr. Edwin McGrue, hovered in his shadow, taking the completed pages of Driscoll's scrawling handwriting from him and laying them aside in a wooden box. (18) Night after night, long after Driscoll had retired for rest, McGrue methodically tossed each page into a roaring fire in his employer's own living room. (19) In time, the madness would pass and Driscoll would became aware of Edwin's deceit. (20) However, by that time, McGrue would be back with the man who had hired him for such a task: Samuel English, creative writer and dialogue magician.

(21) Unfortunately, English's longstanding talent had waned in the past few years and his greatest competition, Evan Driscoll was slated to become the world's most acclaimed author of our time. (22) English's novels had graced the bookstands of stores across the country, but Driscoll was steadily conquering the world. (23) It became Englishs' only desire—far beyond becoming a fine writer—to demolish Driscoll's career.

(24) It was Edwin McGrue's task to pour tinctures into Driscoll's coffee as he worked. (25) These potions would still his thinking processes and drive him to the point of madness, which they were designed to. (26) English had come upon these tinctures from a secretive source hidden in the back allies of Marysport. (27) McGrue remorselessly polluted Driscoll's coffee with these flavorless concoctions.

1. Choose the sentence that could **best** be added right after sentence 27.

   a. McGrue lived in a small apartment.
   b. Driscoll had yet to discover the horrifying truth.
   c. English and Driscoll met in a train station just outside of Marysport.
   d. Frankly, writing was McGrue's most loathsome task.

2. Choose the correct way to write the underlined part of sentence 5.

   "Could it be that I don't <u>write as good as I think I do?"</u>

   a. write as good as I think I do."
   b. write as well as I think I do?"
   c. write as good, as I think I do?"
   d. No change is needed.

3. Choose the correct way to write the underlined part of sentence 23.

   <u>It became Englishs' only desire</u>—far beyond becoming a fine writer—to demolish Driscoll's career.

   a. It became English's only desire
   b. It became Englishs' only deesire.
   c. It become Englishs' only desire
   d. No change is needed.

4. Read sentence 25, which is poorly written.

These potions would still his thinking processes and drive him to the point of madness, which they were designed to.

Choose the **best** way to rewrite this sentence.

a. His thinking processes having been stilled and his madness having been driven, these potions worked as they were designed to.
b. By driving him to the point of madness, these potions were designed to still his thinking processes.
c. These potions were designed to still his thinking processes and drive him to the point of madness.
d. These potions were designed, and stilled his thinking process and drove him to the point of madness.

5. Drew wants to add this sentence to the paragraph that begins with sentence 24.

However, even his shifty companion did not know where he found them— nor did he want to know.

Where would the sentence **best** fit?

a. right after sentence 24
b. right after sentence 25
c. right after sentence 26
d. right after sentence 27

6. Choose the correct way to write the underlined part of sentence 4.

His massive shoulders seemed <u>to swell out from under a undersized overcoat,</u> a relic of a time when men wore suits no matter what their employ.

a. to swell out from under an undersized overcoat,
b. to swelled out from under a undersized overcoat,
c. to swell out, from under a undersized overcoat,
d. No change is needed.

7. Choose the correct way to write the underlined part of sentence 8.

    His hollowed <u>eyes hung loosely in they're sockets,</u> and his cheekbones were sharp points jutting out from a concave face.

    a. eyes hang loosely in they're sockets,
    b. eyes hung loosely in their sockets,
    c. eyes hung losely in they're sockets,
    d. No change is needed.

8. Choose the correct way to write the underlined part of sentence 21.

    Unfortunately, English's longstanding talent had waned in the past few years and his greatest competition, Evan <u>Driscoll was slated to become the world's most acclaimed author of our time.</u>

    a. Driscoll was slated to become the world's most acclaimed author of our time?
    b. Driscoll was slated to become the world's most acclaimed author of hour time.
    c. Driscoll, was slated to become the world's most acclaimed author of our time.
    d. No change is needed.

9. Choose the correct way to write the underlined part of sentence 26.

    English had come upon these tinctures from a secretive source hidden in <u>the back allies of Marysport.</u>

    a. the back allies' of Marysport.
    b. the back alleys of Marysport.
    c. the back allies, of Marysport.
    d. No change is needed.

10. Choose the correct way to write the underlined part of sentence 6.

    "Impossible, Evan," replied a frail man who <u>seemed made of the most thinner crepe.</u>

    a. seemed made of the most thinner Crepe.
    b. seemed made of the most, thinner crepe.
    c. seemed made of the thinnest crepe.
    d. No change is needed.

Julia is in the seventh grade. Her music class is studying classical music, and her teacher asked each student to write a short paper comparing and contrasting the classical and romantic periods in music. Julia took notes from her library books, made an outline, and then wrote her rough draft. Now she needs your help editing and revising it.

Here is Julia's rough draft. Read it and then answer questions 1–10.

(1) Many people think that all music that is not popular music, rock music, or jazz is "classical" music. (2) I used to think so, too. (3) Now I know that what I used to call "classical" music might be either Baroque, Classical, Romantic, or Modern music. (4) Let's take a look at the Classical and Romantic periods in music.

(5) The Classical period lasted from about 1720 to about 1800. (6) The "Enlightenment" was going on in europe at this time. (7) The Enlightenment was a way of thinking about life. (8) People started to believe that the individual person was more important then the government or society. (9) They believed that the answers to all questions could be found in nature, and they believed that knowledge and reason could solve any problem. (10) People valued balance, order, and logic during the Enlightenment.

(11) The Enlightenment influenced music during the Classical period. (12) Composers started trying to write music that was very structured and balanced without being too emotional. (13) People during the Enlightenment believed that all human beings were under the same universal, natural law. (14) Composers in several countries tried to follow the same rules for writing music. (15) Franz Joseph Haydn, Wolfgang Amadeus Mozart and Ludwig van Beethoven were Classical composers.

(16) The Romantic period lasted from about 1800 to World War I. (17) Freedom, movement, and emotion were the most important things to Romantic composers. (18) Composers stopped trying to follow the same rules as everyone else. (19) They started expressing their own emotions in their music they stopped trying so hard to please their "patrons." (20) A patron was a very wealthy person who supported a musician paying money.

(21) During the Romantic period, the middle class became more able to pay for concerts and music lessons. (22) Romantic composers played for large audienses, not just small groups of wealthy patrons. (23) Some of them became as popular as pop stars are to us today. (24) Some Romantic composers were Franz Shubert, Robert Schumann, Johannes Brahms, and Peter Tchaikovsky.

(25) Romantic composers wanted to express their individual creativity, but they did not totally abandon Classical techniques. (26) The music changed quite a bit, but much more radical changes would come later in the twentieth century.

1. The topic sentence of the paragraph that begins with sentence 11 is

   a. sentence 11.
   b. sentence 12.
   c. sentence 14.
   d. sentence 15.

2. Choose the sentence that could **best** be added right after sentence 9.

   a. The Romantic period lasted longer than the Classical period.
   b. Many people became very interested in science.
   c. The Modern movement started around the time of World War I.
   d. Most of the middle class did not have the means to pay for music lessons.

3. Choose the correct way to write the underlined part of sentence 15.

   Franz Joseph Haydn, Wolfgang <u>Amadeus Mozart and Ludwig van Beethoven were Classical</u> composers.

   a. Amadeus Mozart and Ludwig van Beethoven were classical
   b. Amadeus Mozart, and Ludwig van Beethoven were Classical
   c. Amadeus Mozart and Ludwig Van Beethoven was Classical
   d. No change is needed.

4. Choose the correct way to write the underlined part of sentence 21.

   <u>During the Romantic period, the middle class became</u> more able to pay for concerts and music lessons.

   a. During the romantic period, the middle class became
   b. During the Romantic period, the middle class, became
   c. During, the Romantic period, the middle class became
   d. No change is needed.

5. Choose the correct way to write the underlined part of sentence 6.

   The "Enlightenment" was going on in europe at this time.

   a. "Enlightenment," was going on in europe
   b. "enlightenment" was going on in europe
   c. "Enlightenment" was going on in Europe
   d. No change is needed.

6. Read sentence 19, which is poorly written.

   They started expressing their own emotions in their music they stopped trying so hard to please their "patrons."

   Choose the **best** way to rewrite this sentence.

   a. They started expressing their own emotions in their music trying so hard to please their "patrons."
   b. They stopped trying so hard to please their "patrons" so they started expressing their own emotions in their music and they stopped trying so hard.
   c. They started expressing their own emotions. In their music they stopped trying so hard. They stopped trying to please their "patrons."
   d. They started expressing their own emotions in their music, and they stopped trying so hard to please their "patrons."

7. Choose the correct way to write the underlined part of sentence 22.

   Romantic composers played for large audienses, not just small groups of wealthy patrons.

   a. composers played for large audiences,
   b. composers played four large audienses,
   c. composers, played for large audienses,
   d. No change is needed.

8. Julia wants to change sentence 26 so that it is more specific.

   <u>The music changed quite a bit, but much</u> more radical changes would come later in the twentieth century.

   Choose the **best** way to rewrite the underlined part of this sentence.

   a. Although the music changed dramatically, even
   b. The music sounded very different from before, but much
   c. The music became more radical, emotional, but much
   d. The music had some similarities and differences, but much

9. Choose the correct way to write the underlined part of sentence 8.

   People started to believe that the individual person was <u>more important then the government</u> or society.

   a. most important then the government
   b. importanter then the government
   c. more important than the government
   d. No change is needed.

10. Read sentence 20, which is poorly written.

    A patron was a very wealthy person who supported a musician paying money.

    Choose the **best** way to rewrite this sentence.

    a. A patron was a very wealthy person who supported a musician he paid money.
    b. Who supported a musician paying money? A very wealthy person who was a patron.
    c. A patron was a very wealthy person supporting a musician who payed money.
    d. A patron was a very wealthy person who supported a musician with money.

Kyle's seventh-grade class is learning how to write persuasively. Kyle's teacher asked him to think about something that he would like to have and then to write a letter to convince his parents that he deserved it. Kyle has written his rough draft, and now he needs your help editing and revising it.

Here is Kyle's rough draft. Read it and then answer questions 1–10.

(1) Dear Mom and Dad,

(2) I have been thinking a lot about finances lately, and I believe that I deserve a bigger allowance. (3) I know that you don't own the bank and that money doesn't grow on trees, but I believe that I need more money. (4) I will work to deserve the extra money.

(5) One reason that I need more money is that the cost of living has gone up. (6) The school cafeteria just raised its prices on the snacks I like to buy. (7) The fines at the library went up. (8) Movies are more expensive. (9) Even the swimming pool fee at the park has gone up. (10) I am in seventh grade now, so I am eating more than I used to. (11) I'm also doing more things. (12) I like to practice at the batting cages play games at the arcade, and go to the amusement park. (13) I would like to have more of my own money to spend on all these things.

(14) Another reason that I need more money is that I would like to start really saving. (15) Its fun to spend money, but I would like to put more money into my savings account. (16) I know that you think saving money is important. (17) If you gave me a bigger allowance, I would have more money to put into savings.

(18) It wouldn't be fair for me to ask you to give me extra cash every week without giving you something in return. (19) I plan to earn my bigger allowance by doing work for you. (20) You could give me work like mowing the lawn, cleaning the house, babysitting, or doing odd jobs. (21) After all, someday I'm going to have to know how to do it all for myself. (22) If you gave me more work to do. (23) I would learn how to be more responsible. (24) You would have more free time, and I would have more money. (25) Just imagine it!

(26) Please consider giving me a bigger allowance. (27) I hope you agree that it would be well worth the invessment.

(28) Sincerely

(29) Kyle

1. Choose the word or phrase that **best** fits at the beginning of sentence 4.

    a. Therefore,
    b. For example,
    c. All kidding aside,
    d. Next,

2. Choose the correct way to write the underlined part of sentence 12.

    I like to practice at <u>the batting cages play games at the arcade, and</u> go to the amusement park.

    a. the batting cages' play games at the arcade, and
    b. the batting cages play games at the arcade and
    c. the batting cages, play games at the arcade, and
    d. No change is needed.

3. Choose the correct way to write the underlined part of sentence 15.

    <u>Its fun to spend money, but</u> I would like to put more money into my savings account.

    a. Its fun to spend money but
    b. Its fun to spends money, but
    c. It's fun to spend money, but
    d. No change is needed.

4. Which of these is **not** a complete sentence?

    a. I hope you agree that it would be well worth the invessment.
    b. One reason that I need more money is that the cost of living has gone up.
    c. Another reason that I need more money is that I would like to start really saving.
    d. If you gave me more work to do.

5. Choose the correct way to write line 1, the opening of the letter.

Dear Mom and Dad,

    a. Dear Mom and Dad.
    b. Dear mom and dad,
    c. Deer Mom and Dad,
    d. No change is needed.

6. Choose the correct way to write line 28, the closing of the letter.

Sincerely

    a. sincerely
    b. Sinceerly
    c. Sincerely,
    d. No change is needed.

7. Choose the sentence that could **best** be added right after sentence 20.

    a. My sister doesn't know how to do this stuff.
    b. You could teach me how to cook, and I could make dinner sometimes.
    c. It would eat into my television-watching time.
    d. The extra cash would be awfully nice to have.

8. Choose the **best** way to write the underlined part of sentence 9 so that the composition maintains a consistent tone.

Even the swimming pool fee at the park <u>has gone up.</u>

    a. isn't cheap enough.
    b. has increased.
    c. costs a whole lot more.
    d. is way more than I can afford.

9. Read sentence 4, which is poorly written.

    I will work to deserve the extra money.

    Choose the **best** way to rewrite this sentence.

    a. I will earn the extra money I deserve.
    b. I deserve the extra money, and I will work.
    c. I will work, I will get extra money.
    d. I will work to earn the extra money.

10. Choose the correct way to write the underlined part of sentence 27.

    I hope you agree that it <u>would be well worth the invessment.</u>

    a. would be good worth the invessment.
    b. would been well worth the invessment.
    c. would be well worth the investment.
    d. No change is needed.

Alicia is in the seventh grade. Her teacher asked each student to choose one disease that humans can get from insects or animals and write a short report about it. Alicia chose to write about Lyme disease. She took notes, organized them, and wrote her rough draft. Now she needs your help editing and revising it.

Here is Alicia's rough draft. Read it and then answer questions 1–10.

(1) If you live in the northeastern United States, you definitely have heard of Lyme disease. (2) Before 1977, nobody knew about Lyme disease. (3) Then, a group of children in the town of Lyme Connecticut, started developing painful arthritis. (4) When scientists investigated, they found that all the children had been infected with a bacterium, *Borrelia burgdorferi*. (5) They found that people were getting this bacterium by being bitten by deer ticks.

(6) The deer ticks that carry the infection are much smaller than ordinary ticks found on some animals. (7) They feed by inserting there mouths into the skin of their hosts and slowly taking in the hosts' blood. (8) A tick can feed on its host for several days. (9) The longer it keeps feeding, the more likely it is to transmit Lyme disease.

(10) The symptoms of Lyme disease include a round, red rash at the site of the bite, headaches, fever, and pain in the joints and muscles. (11) Sometimes people with Lyme disease have a lot of itching. (12) Some people develop heart problems or neurological problems.

(13) The people most at risk for getting Lyme disease are those living in the northeastern states. (14) However, there have been some cases in the mid-atlantic states and parts of California, too. (15) People who spend a lot of time outdoors are at higher risk than those who don't. (16) People who go in the woods a lot are especially at risk.

(17) What if you love hiking and camping! (18) It's not always possible to avoid places where there are deer ticks. (19) There are things you can do to keep from getting Lyme disease. (20) You can wear long-sleeved shirts and tuck your pants into you're socks. (21) You can wear light-colored clothes so that you can see ticks that jump on you. (22) If you have exposed skin, you can apply insect repellent that contains DEET. (23) You can apply permethrin to your clothes, too. (24) Permethrin kills ticks on contact. (25) Probably the most important thing is to do a daily tick check. (26) If you can find a tick that has been there for just a day and remove it with tweezers. (27) You probably will not get Lyme disease.

(28) If you do get Lyme disease, you should get started on antibiotics immediately. (29) If you catch them early, Lyme disease can be cured.

1. Choose the correct way to write the underlined part of sentence 14.

    However, there have been some cases in the mid-atlantic states and parts of **California, too.**

    a. However, there has been some cases in the mid-atlantic states
    b. However there have been some cases in the mid-atlantic states
    c. However, there have been some cases in the mid-Atlantic states
    d. No change is needed.

2. Alicia wants to change sentence 6 so that it is more specific.

    The deer ticks that carry the infection are much smaller than ordinary ticks found on some animals.

    Choose the **best** way to rewrite the underlined part of this sentence.

    a. on farms.
    b. on dogs, cats, and cattle.
    c. on various animals around town.
    d. in the summer.

3. Choose the correct way to write the underlined part of sentence 29.

    If you catch them early, Lyme disease can be cured.

    a. catch them early, lyme disease
    b. catch it early, Lyme disease
    c. catches them early, Lyme disease
    d. No change is needed.

4. Choose the correct way to write the underlined part of sentence 3.

    Then, a group of children in the town of Lyme Connecticut, started developing painful arthritis.

    a. children in the town, of Lyme Connecticut,
    b. children in the town of Lyme and Connecticut,
    c. children in the town of Lyme, Connecticut,
    d. No change is needed.

5. Choose the correct way to write the underlined part of sentence 20.

   You can wear long-sleeved shirts and <u>tuck your pants into you're socks.</u>

   a. tuck your pants into your socks.
   b. tucked your pants into you're socks.
   c. tuck your pants, into you're socks.
   d. No change is needed.

6. Choose the **best** way to combine the ideas in sentences 15 and 16 into one sentence.

   People who spend a lot of time outdoors are at higher risk than those who don't. People who go in the woods a lot are especially at risk.

   a. People who spend a lot of time outdoors are at higher risk, but so are people who go in the woods.
   b. People who go in the woods and spend time outdoors are especially at risk.
   c. By going in the woods and spending time outdoors, the risks are especially high, but especially if you spend a lot of time in the woods.
   d. People who spend a lot of time outdoors, especially in the woods, are at higher risk than those who don't.

7. Choose the correct way to write the underlined part of sentence 7.

   They feed by inserting <u>there mouths into the skin of their hosts</u> and slowly taking in the hosts' blood.

   a. there mouths into the skin of their host's
   b. there mouth's into the skin of their hosts
   c. their mouths into the skin of their hosts
   d. No change is needed.

8. Which of these is **not** a complete sentence?

   a. If you can find a tick that has been there for just a day and remove it with tweezers.
   b. A tick can feed on its host for several days.
   c. Before 1977, nobody knew about Lyme disease.
   d. Some people develop heart problems or neurological problems.

9. Choose the correct way to write the underlined part of sentence 17.

    What if <u>you love hiking and camping!</u>

    a. you love hiking, and camping!
    b. me love hiking and camping!
    c. you love hiking and camping?
    d. No change is needed.

10. Read sentence 11, which is poorly written.

    Sometimes people with Lyme disease have a lot of itching.

    Choose the **best** way to rewrite this sentence.

    a. Sometimes, when there's itching, people have Lyme disease.
    b. Sometimes, people with Lyme disease become very itchy.
    c. Even if it's a lot of itching, Lyme disease comes with people.
    d. Sometimes, people with Lyme disease have a bunch of itching.

Jacob is in the seventh grade. His geography teacher asked each student to choose a country and to write a short report describing the land and the people there. Jacob chose to write about South Korea. He researched his subject, organized his notes, and wrote his rough draft. Now he needs your help editing and revising it.

Here is Jacob's rough draft. Read it and then answer questions 1–10.

(1) The Republic of Korea is commonly known as South Korea. (2) It is located in the southern half of the Korean peninsula in East Asia. (3) The Democratic Republic of Korea which lies to the north, is known as North Korea. (4) These two countries used to be a single nation. (5) Then, in 1948, the world's superpowers divided the country into a communist North and non-communist South. (6) The capital of South Korea is Seoul, and it is also the largest city in the country. (7) In the year 2000, there were 10.4 million people living in Seoul, which makes it the most populated city in the world (if you don't count major metropolitan areas.)

(8) The Korean peninsula is located between the Yellow Sea and the Sea of Japan. (9) The east china sea lies to the south. (10) The southeastern landscape is very dramatic. (11) It has mountain ranges that have deep, narrow valleys between them. (12) The southwestern part of the country is mostly coastal plains, and this is where most of the people live.

(13) South Korea has a temperate climate, but sometimes it gets bitterly cold during the winter. (14) There is a short rainy season every summer.

(15) The Korean population is one of the least diferce groups of people in the world. (16) Except for a small Chinese community, most people in Korea are of the same ethnic group and speak the same language. (17) Koreans have friendly relationships with the United States and Canada. (18) Many Koreans who leave their country choose to come to North America.

(19) The Korean language has a writing system that is unique. (20) In 1446, King Sejong the Great invented it and called it the "Hangul." (21) In this system, words are spelled exactly as they sound. (22) While Japan ruled Korea, people were forbidden to write or speak the Korean language. (23) Still, the language survived. (24) Today, English is taught as a second language in most Korean schools. (25) When Korean students get to high school, they can study Chinese, Japanese, French, German or Spanish.

(26) The two most popular religions in South Korea are Christianity and Buddhism. (27) Before 1970, Buddhism dominated, but Christianity has overtaken it in recent years. (28) About thirty-five percent of South Koreans say they follow no particular religion.

(29) In the last few years, South Korea and North Korea had considering reunification. (30) I wonder what'll happen.

1. Choose the correct way to write the underlined part of sentence 15.

   The Korean population is one of the <u>least diferce groups of people in the world.</u>

   a. least diferce groups of people in the World.
   b. least diverse groups of people in the world.
   c. least diferce group's of people in the world.
   d. No change is needed.

2. Choose the correct way to write the underlined part of sentence 25.

   When Korean students <u>get to high school, they can study Chinese, Japanese, French, German or Spanish.</u>

   a. get to High School, they can study Chinese, Japanese, French, German or Spanish.
   b. get to high school, they can study Chinese, Japanese, French, German, or Spanish.
   c. goes to high school, they can study Chinese, Japanese, French, German or Spanish.
   d. No change is needed.

3. Choose the word or phrase that **best** fits at the beginning of sentence 18.

   a. Nevertheless,
   b. However,
   c. Then,
   d. In fact,

4. Read sentence 12, which is poorly written.

    The southwestern part of the country is mostly coastal plains, and this is where most of the people live.

    Choose the **best** way to rewrite this sentence.

    a. The southwestern part of the country, where mostly coastal plains are, is where most people live.
    b. People mainly live in the southwestern part of the country, which is mostly coastal plains.
    c. Coastal plains and people live in the southwestern part of the country.
    d. The country contains both coastal plains and people mostly in its southwestern part.

5. Read sentence 19, which is poorly written.

    The Korean language has a writing system that is unique.

    Choose the **best** way to rewrite this sentence.

    a. The Korean language is a writing system, which is unique.
    b. The unique writing system of the Koreans can be found in their language.
    c. The Korean language has a unique writing system.
    d. A writing system from the Korean language is unique.

6. Choose the correct way to write the underlined part of sentence 3.

    The <u>Democratic Republic of Korea which lies</u> to the north, is known as North Korea.

    a. democratic republic of Korea which lies
    b. Democratic Republic of Korea which lays
    c. Democratic Republic of Korea, which lies
    d. No change is needed.

7. Choose the correct way to write the underlined part of sentence 9.

   The east china sea lies to the south.

   a. The East China sea lies
   b. The East China Sea lies
   c. The china sea lies east
   d. No change is needed.

8. Choose the **best** way to write the underlined part of sentence 30 so that the composition maintains a consistent tone.

   I wonder what'll happen.

   a. It will be interesting to see if these two countries ever join together again.
   b. I seriously doubt that will happen, but we'll see.
   c. South Korea and North Korea getting along? C'mon!
   d. It sounds like they've got a lot of problems to resolve first, though.

9. Choose the correct way to write the underlined part of sentence 7.

   In the year 2000, there were 10.4 million people living in Seoul, which makes it the most populated city in the world (if you don't count major metropolitan areas.)

   a. in the world (if you don't count major, metropolitan areas.)
   b. in the world (if you don't count major metropolitan areas).
   c. in the world: (if you don't count major metropolitan areas.)
   d. No change is needed.

10. Choose the correct way to write the underlined part of sentence 29.

    In the last few years, South Korea and North Korea had considering reunification.

    a. South Korea and North Korea had conssidering
    b. south Korea and north Korea had considering
    c. South Korea and North Korea have been considering
    d. No change is needed.

Tamara's seventh-grade class is getting ready to vote to elect new officers for the Student Government Association. Her teacher asked each student to choose one candidate and to write a letter to convince the class to vote for him or her. Tamara has written a rough draft of her letter, and now she needs your help editing and revising it.

Here is Tamara's rough draft. Read it and then answer questions 1–10.

(1) Dear Fellow Classmates,

(2) It is that time of year again: class elections! (3) Have you decided whom you're voting for yet? (4) If not, please consider voting for Stephanie Hernandez. (5) There are many reasons why Stephanie is my favorite candidate.

(6) Stephanie is, above all, a leader. (7) She is not a follower of the crowd. (8) Whenever people are doing something Stephanie doesn't think is right, she always tells them that to their faces. (9) Whenever there is a chance to take charge, you will find Stephanie in the center of the action. (10) She is the captain of the girl's basketball team. (11) She also helps teach young children at her church. (12) She has long brown hair. (13) She has school spirit, too. (14) She is the person who thought of the design for our school anniversary pin.

(15) Stephanie genuinely cares about other people. (16) People go to Stephanie with their problems. (17) They know she will listen and won't laugh at them. (18) Her advice is usually very good, too. (19) Stephanie does not play favorites or treat other people unfairly. (20) If anyone needs a helping hand, she is always the first one ready to offer her help. (21) When a student is out sick, Stephanie collects all the work, than explains it to the student when he or she comes back.

(22) I think Stephanie has another important quality that leaders need, and that's humility. (23) If she scores the most points in a game, she doesn't boast about it to everyone and say, "Look how great I am!" (24) When she is defeated, she accepts it with grace and dignity. (25) If somebody else doesn't do good, she encourages the person. (26) "Don't worry, I'm sure you'll do better next time" she will say. (27) It's no wonder Stephanie has a lot of friends. (28) She makes the people around her feel good.

(29) When it is time to cast your vote for class president on Tuesday, I hope you will remember the name Stephanie Hernandez. (30) When it comes to representing our class, I know she will do the best possible job.

(31) Sincerely

(32) Tamara Leonardo

1. Choose the correct way to write the underlined part of sentence 21.

   When a student is out sick, Stephanie collects all the work, <u>than explains it to the student when he or she comes back.</u>

   a. than explains it to the student when he or she came back.
   b. then explains it to the student when he or she comes back.
   c. than explains it to the student, when he or she comes back.
   d. No change is needed.

2. Choose the sentence that does **not** belong in the paragraph that begins with sentence 6.

   a. sentence 6
   b. sentence 8
   c. sentence 9
   d. sentence 12

3. Choose the correct way to write the underlined part of sentence 26.

   <u>"Don't worry, I'm sure you'll do better next time"</u> she will say.

   a. "Don't worry, I'm sure you've do better next time"
   b. "Don't worry, I'm sure you'll do better next time,"
   c. "don't worry, I'm sure you'll do better next time"
   d. No change is needed.

4. Choose the sentence that could **best** be added right after sentence 2.

   a. Deciding whom to elect for class president this year is going to be tough.
   b. I've made all my decisions already.
   c. The most popular kids always win.
   d. Student Government will be holding meetings every other Thursday.

5. Choose the correct way to write the underlined part of sentence 29.

When it is time to cast your vote for class president on Tuesday, I hope you will remember the name Stephanie Hernandez.

   a.   will remember the Name Stephanie Hernandez.
   b.   will remembers the name Stephanie Hernandez.
   c.   will remember the name Stephanie Hernandez?
   d.   No change is needed.

6. Choose the **best** way to write the underlined part of sentence 8 so that the composition maintains a consistent tone.

Whenever people are doing something Stephanie doesn't think is right, she always tells them that to their faces.

   a.   she tells them straight out what's wrong with what they are doing.
   b.   she is not afraid to speak her mind about it.
   c.   she isn't afraid of people not doing the wrong thing.
   d.   she's been known to not do the right thing from time to time.

7. Choose the correct way to write line 31, the closing of the letter.

Sincerely

   a.   Sinsereley
   b.   sincerely
   c.   Sincerely,
   d.   No change is needed.

8. Choose the **best** way to combine the ideas in sentences 16 and 17 into one sentence.

People go to Stephanie with their problems. They know she will listen and won't laugh at them.

    a. Stephanie is often told people's problems and she listens and she doesn't laugh.
    b. People tell Stephanie their problems knowing very well that she won't listen or laugh.
    c. People's problems are especially important to Stephanie to help her listen and laugh.
    d. People go to Stephanie with their problems because they know she will listen and not laugh.

9. Choose the correct way to write the underlined part of sentence 25.

If somebody <u>else doesn't do good, she encourages</u> the person.

    a. else, doesn't do good, she encourages
    b. else doesn't do well, she encourages
    c. else doesn't do good, she encourajes
    d. No change is needed.

10. Choose the correct way to write the underlined part of sentence 10.

She is the <u>captain of the girl's basketball</u> team.

    a. Captain of the girl's basketball
    b. captain of the Girl's basketball
    c. captain of the girls' basketball
    d. No change is needed.

Simon has been asked by his seventh-grade teacher to write a convincing article in favor of spaying and neutering pets. This topic is something Simon feels strongly about, so he enthusiastically begins gathering information and visiting local shelters. He has taken extensive notes and written his rough draft. He needs your help editing it.

Here is Simon's rough draft. Read it and then answer questions 1–10.

(1) Not enough people understand the cat and dog overpopulation crisis going on in the United States today. (2) The shelters in this country are overloaded with household pets that people have given up or abandoned. (3) Shelters do their best to support and maintain successful facilities. (4) The staff wants nothing more then to find good homes for all the animals in their care. (5) However, it would be a miracle if they could save every animal that crosses their path. (6) One effective solution to this problem is spaying and neutering pets.

(7) People often treat their pets as material possessions instead of living things. (8) Pet owners' common excuses for not spaying or neutering their pets is that they have not bothered to do it yet. (9) What a shame! (10) Domestic animals are given up to shelters for too many reasons. (11) Perhaps the owners were moving, a landlord would not allow pets, or there were too many animals already in the household. (12) Maybe the pet cost too much to take care of, the owner was having personal problems, or he or she did not have adequate facilities for the pet. (13) Sometimes people say really dumb stuff like they don't want to pay to board the animal while on vacation.

(14) No matter what the excuse domestic animals are being "euthanized," or killed, every day. (15) At least 10 to 12 million animals are euthanized each year because there aren't enough homes for them. (16) As many as a million animals a month. (17) Unfortunately, shelters just cannot handle the influx of pets they receive.

(18) The statistical data surrounding pet overpopulation in this country is shocking. (19) If an unaltered cat, for example, is living on the street, he will most likely reproduce at will. (20) In fact, two unaltered cats and all of their desendants can theoretically number 450,000 cats total in just seven years. (21) One unspayed female dog and her offspring can produce 67,000 dogs in just six years.

(22) Kittens and puppies are often taken to shelters because breeders were unable to find homes for the littermates. (23) Many animals are simply neglected or abandoned by their owners or run away. (24) Over half of the dogs and a little less than half of the cats of the shelter population come to the facility unaltered. (25) As many as 25% of shelter animals are purebreds. (26) The owners would have paid good money to get a purebred animal. (27) Why would they toss it away?

(28) Perhaps more people would spay and neuter their animals if they knew the health benefits to the pet. (29) The simple truth is that pet owners should know the dreadful consequences of the pet overpopulation problem. (30) Not spaying or neutering animals is the main cause. (31) Educate yourself and those around you about responsible pet ownership and the importance of spaying and neutering. (32) The information will save lives!

49

1. Choose the correct way to write the underlined part of sentence 20.

   In fact, two unaltered cats and <u>all of their desendants can theoretically</u> number 450,000 cats total in just seven years.

   a. all of they're desendants can theoretically
   b. all of their descendants can theoretically
   c. all of their desendants are theoretically
   d. No change is needed.

2. Read sentence 23, which is poorly written.

   Many animals are simply neglected or abandoned by their owners or run away.

   Choose the **best** way to rewrite this sentence.

   a. Many animals are simply neglected, abandoned, run away from their owners.
   b. Many animals run away because they are simply abandoned by their owners.
   c. Many animals simply run away or are neglected or abandoned by their owners.
   d. Many animals abandon and neglect their owners because they ran away.

3. The topic sentence of the paragraph that begins with sentence 7 is

   a. sentence 7.
   b. sentence 10.
   c. sentence 11.
   d. sentence 13.

4. Choose the correct way to write the underlined part of sentence 14.

   No matter what the <u>excuse domestic animals are being "euthanized,"</u> or killed, every day.

   a. excuse, domestic animals are being "euthanized,"
   b. excuse domestic animals is being "euthanized,"
   c. excuse domestic animals are being "Euthanized,"
   d. No change is needed.

5. Choose the correct way to write the underlined part of sentence 4.

   The staff wants nothing more <u>then to find good homes</u> for all the animals in their care.

   a. then to find good homes'
   b. than to find good homes
   c. then to find well homes
   d. No change is needed.

6. Which of these is **not** a complete sentence?

   a. Why would they toss it away?
   b. Maybe the pet cost too much to take care of, the owner was having personal problems, or he or she did not have adequate facilities for the pet.
   c. The information will save lives!
   d. As many as a million animals a month.

7. Choose the word or phrase that **best** fits at the beginning of sentence 25.

   a. Surprisingly,
   b. Fortunately,
   c. Nevertheless,
   d. For instance,

8. Choose the **best** way to write the underlined part of sentence 13 so that the composition maintains a consistent tone.

   <u>Sometimes people say really dumb stuff like they don't want to</u> pay to board the animal while on vacation.

   a. It's incredible what some people come up with when they want to go on vacation, like saying they don't want to
   b. Sometimes, people will act like they don't even care when they're going away and they'll tell you they don't want to
   c. Some people surrender their pets for more thoughtless reasons, such as not wanting to
   d. Can you believe some of these excuses, like saying you don't want to

9. Simon wants to add this sentence to the paragraph that begins with sentence 28.

   Dogs and cats have a greatly improved chance of living long, healthy, contented lives if they are spayed and neutered.

   Where would the sentence **best** fit?

   a. right after sentence 28
   b. right after sentence 29
   c. right after sentence 31
   d. right after sentence 32

10. Choose the correct way to write the underlined part of sentence 22.

   Kittens and puppies are often taken to shelters <u>because breeders were unable to find homes</u> for the littermates.

   a. because breeders were unable to find home's
   b. because breeders are unable to find homes
   c. because, breeders were unable to find homes
   d. No change is needed.

Jackson's seventh-grade history teacher asked the class to draw a parallel between something they are interested in and their studies of the sixteenth century. Jackson makes a discovery, does some research, makes an outline for his report, and writes his rough draft. He needs your help editing and revising it.

Here is Jackson's rough draft. Read it and then answer questions 1–10.

(1) *Calvin and Hobbes* is one of the best known comic strips of the last twenty-five years. (2) Written and illustrated by Bill Watterson from 1985 to 1995, it was carried in over 2,400 newspapers. (3) But did you know that Calvin, the six-year-old boy in the strip, is named after sixteenth-century theologian John Calvin?

(4) John Calvin was born on July 10, 1509, in Noyon France. (5) He was raised in a strict Roman Catholic family. (6) In fact, John's fathers' work in the local cathedral led him to want John to be a priest.

(7) Calvin traveled to Paris to study at the College de Marche when he was fourteen years old. (8) He studied just seven subjects: rhetoric (public speaking), geometry, arithmetic, astronomy, music, logic, and grammar. (9) While living in Paris, he changed his name to Ioannis Calvinus, the latin form of John Calvin. (10) (In French, his name is Jean Calvin.)

(11) By 1532, Calvin had published his first book, a commentary on *De Clementia* by Roman philosopher Seneca. (12) He had also made friends with some reformist individuals, who, at the time, who were seeking change. (13) Soon thereafter, he fled Paris because of ties with those same reformers, who were becoming known for lecturing and writing against the Roman Catholic Church.

(14) For three years following his departure from Paris, Calvin lived in various places under various names. (15) He studied and preached. (16) He began work on the first edition of the *Institutes of the Christian Religion*. (17) That book made him famous. (18) With this book, he permanently seperated himself from the Roman Catholic Church. (19) Calvin's writings would spread the ideas of "Calvinism" throughout Europe and even across the Atlantic to the New World. (20) Soon, countries around the world would be learning and adopting Calvinist principles.

(21) Calvin was passing through Geneva when he was met by William Farel, a local reformer. (22) Farel invited Calvin to stay in Geneva and, sources say, threatened him with God's anger if he did not. (23) However, many people disagreed with Calvin's theological viewpoints and the changes he and Farel had set out to make. (24) In 1538, both Calvin and his partner were asked to leave.

(25) After moving to Strasbourg, Calvin was surprised when the Council of Geneva, in 1541, requested that he return to Geneva. (26) He did, eventually, return and began work as a lecturer, preacher, and writer of commentaries, treatises, and further

(continued on next page)

(continued from previous page)

editions of the *Institutes of the Christian Religion*. (27) He founded a school for training children and a hospital for the needy.

(28) Calvin was not well liked by some and he was sometimes threatened or abused. (29) Later in life, Calvin suffered migraines, lung hemorrhages, gout, and kidney stones. (30) He sometimes had to be carried to the pulpit. (31) When his friends worried him about the amount of work he insisted on doing, Calvin responded, "What! (32) Would you have the Lord find me idle when He comes"?

(33) John Calvin died on May 27, 1564. (34) At his own request he was buried in a simple, unmarked grave somewhere in Geneva.

1. Choose the correct way to write the underlined part of sentence 9.

   While living in Paris, he changed his <u>name to Ioannis Calvinus, the latin</u> form of John Calvin.

   a. name to Ioannis Calvinus the latin
   b. name to Ioannis Calvinus, the Latin
   c. name to, Ioannis Calvinus, the latin
   d. No change is needed.

2. Choose the **best** way to combine the ideas in sentences 15, 16, and 17 into one sentence.

   He studied and preached. He began work on the first edition of the *Institutes of the Christian Religion*. That book made him famous.

   a. He began work on the first edition of the *Institutes of the Christian Religion* that made him famous while he was studying and preaching.
   b. He studied and preached, he finished writing the *Institutes of the Christian Religion* that made him famous.
   c. The *Institutes of the Christian Religion* would make him famous, but he studied and preached, too.
   d. He studied, preached, and began work on the first edition of the *Institutes of the Christian Religion*, the book that made him famous.

3. Choose the correct way to write the underlined part of sentence 32.

Would you have <u>the Lord find me idle when He comes</u>"?

   a. the Lord found me idle when He comes"?
   b. the Lord find me idle when He comes?"
   c. the Lord find me idol when He comes"?
   d. No change is needed.

4. Choose the correct way to write the underlined part of sentence 4.

John Calvin was born on <u>July 10, 1509, in Noyon France.</u>

   a. July 10, 1509, in Noyon, France.
   b. July 10 1509, in Noyon France.
   c. July 10, 1509, in Noyon france.
   d. No change is needed.

5. Read sentence 12, which is poorly written.

He had also made friends with some reformist individuals, who, at the time, who were seeking change.

   Choose the **best** way to rewrite this sentence.

   a. He had made also some friends who were reformists and individuals that had changed.
   b. He and his friends were seeking change in a reformist way at the time.
   c. He had also made friends with some reformist individuals who seek change.
   d. He had also made friends with some individuals who were seeking change, called "reformists."

6. Choose the correct way to write the underlined part of sentence 6.

In fact, <u>John's fathers' work in the local cathedral</u> led him to want John to be a priest.

   a. John's fathers' work in the local Cathedral
   b. John's fathers' worked in the local cathedral
   c. John's father's work in the local cathedral
   d. No change is needed.

7. Choose the correct way to write the underlined part of sentence 3.

   But did you know that Calvin, the six-year-old boy in the strip, <u>is named after sixteenth-century theologian John Calvin?</u>

   a. is named after sixteenth-century theologian John Calvin.
   b. is named after Sixteenth-Century theologian John Calvin?
   c. is named after sixteenth-century theologians John Calvin?
   d. No change is needed.

8. Choose the correct way to write the underlined part of sentence 34.

   <u>At his own request he was buried</u> in a simple, unmarked grave somewhere in Geneva.

   a. At his own request he were buried
   b. At his own request, he was buried
   c. At his own request he was bury
   d. No change is needed.

9. Choose the sentence that could **best** be added right after sentence 22.

   a. Calvin had not planned on staying, but felt that Farel's request was God's intervention.
   b. Calvin's father had told him later on in life to give up theology and turn to the study of law.
   c. Growing up in the presence of the local bishop and his family exposed Calvin to both the aristocracy and culture.
   d. While in Strasbourg, Calvin was quite content working among French Huguenots.

10. Choose the correct way to write the underlined part of sentence 18.

    With this book, he permanently <u>seperated himself from the Roman Catholic Church.</u>

    a. seperated himself from the roman Catholic Church.
    b. seperated himself, from the Roman Catholic Church.
    c. separated himself from the Roman Catholic Church.
    d. No change is needed.

Juan's seventh-grade science class is learning about space travel. His social studies teacher asked each student to form an opinion about whether or not the United States should try to send people to Mars, and then to write a letter to the president to convince him to either accept or reject the idea.

Here is Juan's rough draft. Read it and then answer questions 1–10.

(1) Dear Mr. President,

(2) Space travel has always fascinated we Americans. (3) When Neil Armstrong of the *apollo 11* mission became the first person to step out of his ship and walk on the moon, he called it a "giant leap" for all humankind. (4) Now it seems like everyone is talking about putting people on Mars. (5) Some people even think that there will someday be a colony on Mars. (6) Others believe that it is not wise to spend so much money on a Mars mission when there are so many problems in the world. (7) I think that a Mars mission is well worth the time and money.

(8) A mission to put people on Mars would be good for the world. (9) If we finally did get to the, "red planet," we would learn things that we might never learn if we tried to study the planet from a distance. (10) No one knows the incredible things that might be discovered by astronaut scientists if they could finally dig samples with their own hands. (11) Maybe they would find fossils and other evidence of life among the dust and rocks. (12) Who knows? (13) There could be valyable things on Mars that we humans could use for energy or medicine. (14) If we learned how to live on Mars, it could become a place where humans could go to live if anything ever happened to our own planet.

(15) If you think a mission to Mars would be impossible think again. (16) A team of astronauts could launch their spaceship from the International Space Station. (17) Then, they would land on a satellite orbiting Mars. (18) From there, they would land on a station that would be waiting for them on the surface of the planet. (19) Other spaceships would have been already delivered packages of food and water. (20) The astronauts could dig wells for more water beneath the surface of Mars, and they could use solar panels for electricity. (21) Plants for food could grow inside the station greenhouse.

(22) It is true that sending people to Mars would cost a lot of money. (23) It is true that there are lots of things we have to deal with in the world. (24) However, these problems are very complex, and money is not always the best answer. (25) You're wrong if you don't think we should learn everything we can about Mars. (26) Someday, our lives just may depend on it.

(27) Sincerely,

(28) Juan Martinez

1. Choose the correct way to write the underlined part of sentence 19.

   Other spaceships <u>would have been already delivered packages</u> of food and water.

   a. would have been already deliver packages
   b. would have been already delivered package
   c. would have already delivered packages
   d. No change is needed.

2. Choose the correct way to write the underlined part of sentence 3.

   When Neil Armstrong of <u>the *apollo 11* mission became the first person to step out of his ship</u> and walk on the moon, he called it a "giant leap" for all humankind.

   a. the *Apollo 11* mission became the first person to step out of his ship
   b. the *apollo 11* mission became the first person to step out of his ship,
   c. the *apollo 11* mission, became the first person to step out of his ship
   d. No change is needed.

3. The paragraph that begins with sentence 15 is poorly written. Choose the **best** way to rewrite sentence 18 so that the paragraph does not repeat ideas.

   From there, they would land on a station that would be waiting for them on the surface of the planet.

   a. They would land on a station that would be waiting, but from there they would go to the surface of the planet.
   b. They would land on the surface of the planet on a station that had been waiting for them.
   c. From there, they would get to the surface of the planet and they would find a station waiting there.
   d. From there, they would travel to a station waiting for them on the planet's surface.

4. Juan wants to change sentence 23 so that it is more specific.

    It is true that there <u>are lots of things we have to deal with</u> in the world.

    Choose the **best** way to rewrite the underlined part of this sentence.

    a. are problems
    b. are tons of things to worry about
    c. is war, hunger, and disease
    d. are things that should trouble us

5. Choose the correct way to write the underlined part of sentence 13.

    <u>There could be valyable things on Mars</u> that we humans could use for energy or medicine.

    a. There could be valyable things on mars
    b. Their could be valyable things on Mars
    c. There could be valuable things on Mars
    d. No change is needed.

6. Choose the **best** way to write the underlined part of sentence 25 so that the composition maintains a consistent tone.

    <u>You're wrong if you don't think we should</u> learn everything we can about Mars.

    a. Just because you're President of the United States doesn't mean you decide if we
    b. I think it would be tragic to pass up the opportunity to
    c. We should study up on Mars to
    d. To protect ourselves against alien invasion, we should

7. Choose the correct way to write the underlined part of sentence 2.

    Space travel has always <u>fascinated we Americans.</u>

    a. fascinated us Americans.
    b. fassinated we Americans.
    c. fascinated we americans.
    d. No change is needed.

8. Choose the correct way to write the underlined part of sentence 9.

   If we finally did <u>get to the, "red planet," we would learn things</u> that we would might learn if we tried to study the planet from a distance.

   a. get to the, "red planet," we would learned things
   b. get to the "red planet," we would learn things
   c. get to the, "red planet," we would learn thing's
   d. No change is needed.

9. Choose the correct way to write the underlined part of sentence 15.

   If you think a mission to Mars <u>would be impossible think again.</u>

   a. would have been impossible think again.
   b. would be impossible think again?
   c. would be impossible, think again.
   d. No change is needed.

10. Read sentence 10, which is poorly written.

    No one knows the incredible things that might be discovered by astronaut scientists if they could finally dig samples with their own hands.

    Choose the **best** way to rewrite this sentence.

    a. By digging samples with their own hands, astronaut scientists might be discovered.
    b. Astronaut scientists might make discoveries with their own hands, but no one knows how incredible.
    c. Making discoveries, digging samples, and not knowing are all the incredible things that might happen if astronaut scientists use their own hands.
    d. If astronaut scientists could finally dig samples with their own hands, incredible things might be discovered.

Trent's seventh-grade earth science class is studying scientific theories. His teacher asks each student to write a report on a topic that particularly interests him or her. Trent chooses the "hollow Earth" theory. He visits his school library and writes his first draft. He needs your help editing it.

Here is Trent's rough draft. Read it and then answer questions 1–10.

(1) British astronomer Edmund Halley is usually mentioned in connection with the comet that was named after he, Halley's Comet. (2) Halley had some interesting theories as well. (3) Studying variations in the Earth's magnetic field led him to believe that there were several magnetic fields. (4) He thought that within the hollow Earth were four spheres. (5) One within the other and each with its own magnetic field. (6) Halley also believed that living creatures were inside this hollow globe. (7) He thought that the *aurora borealis*, or northern lights was created by the escape of a glowing atmosphere through a thin crust at the North and South Poles. (8) He proposing these ideas in 1692.

(9) American John Symmes also supported this idea. (10) He was a former army officer and businessman. (11) He believed that the Earth was hollow. (12) He also believed that there were four- to six-thousand-mile-wide entrances inside at the North and South Poles. (13) He raised money to make a expedition to the North Pole to explore the inner Earth, but he was unsuccessful. (14) After Symmes's death, a newspaper editor named Jeremiah Reynolds helped to influence the U.S. government's decision to make such an expedition to Antarctica in 1838. (15) (This expeditions' findings did not support the hollow Earth theory, but did lead explorers to conclude that Antarctica was the world's seventh continent.)

(16) Cyrus Read Teed first introduced the idea of human beings living within the hollow Earth. (17) He proposed that at the center of the hollow sphere was the sun, which was half-dark and half-light. (18) As the sun turned, it gave the appearance of sunrise and sunset. (19) The atmosphere in the center of the sphere was dense. (20) Teed eventually changing his name to "Koresh" and founded what was essentially a cult. (21) He called himself the messiah of a new religion, but died in 1908 without proving any of his ideas.

(22) Even as late as World War II, Adolph Hitler may have sent an expedition to the Baltic Island of Rugen because of these ideas. (23) Once there, a scientist was told to point a telescopic camera into the sky to try to photograph the British fleet across the Earth's hollow center. (24) (He was apparently unsuccessful). (25) *UFOs—Nazi Secret Weapons?* was written by Ernst Zundel. (26) He suggested that nazis came from the inner Earth. (27) Zundel reported that Hitler went in a submarine to the South Pole where he established a base for "flying saucers" in the hole leading inside the Earth.

(28) Over time, new findings have made the hollow Earth theory seem silly. (29) U.S. Navy Admiral Richard Byrd flew across the North Pole in 1926. (30) He didn't see any holes. (31) Then, he flew across the South Pole in 1929. (32) He didn't see any holes then either. (33) In addition, astronauts' photographs show no openings at either spot.

61

1. Trent wants to add this sentence to the paragraph that begins with sentence 16.

   Therefore, people on one side of the world could not see those on the other side.

   Where would the sentence **best** fit?

   a. right after sentence 17
   b. right after sentence 18
   c. right after sentence 19
   d. right after sentence 20

2. Choose the correct way to write the underlined part of sentence 26.

   He suggested that <u>nazis came from the inner</u> Earth.

   a. nazis came from the Inner
   b. nazis came from, the inner
   c. Nazis came from the inner
   d. No change is needed.

3. Choose the correct way to write the underlined part of sentence 8.

   <u>He proposing these ideas</u> in 1692.

   a. He proposed these ideas
   b. He propossing these ideas
   c. Him proposing these ideas
   d. No change is needed.

4. Choose the correct way to write the underlined part of sentence 24.

   (He was <u>apparently unsuccessful).</u>

   a. aparently unsuccessful).
   b. apparently unsuccessful.)
   c. apparently, unsuccessful).
   d. No change is needed.

5. Choose the correct way to write the underlined part of sentence 7.

   He thought that the _aurora borealis, or northern lights was created_ by the escape of a glowing atmosphere through a thin crust at the North and South Poles.

   a. _aurora borealis_, and northern lights was created
   b. _aurora borealis_, or northern lights, was created
   c. _aurora borealis_, or northern lights was create
   d. No change is needed.

6. Which of these is **not** a complete sentence?

   a. He didn't see any holes.
   b. Teed eventually changing his name to "Koresh" and founded what was essentially a cult.
   c. He also believed that there were four- to six-thousand-mile-wide entrances inside at the North and South Poles.
   d. One within the other and each with its own magnetic field.

7. Choose the correct way to write the underlined part of sentence 15.

   (This expeditions' findings did not support the hollow Earth theory, but did lead explorers to conclude that Antarctica was the world's seventh continent.)

   a. (This expedition's findings did not support
   b. (This expeditions' findings did unsupport
   c. (This expeditions' finding's did not support
   d. No change is needed.

8. Choose the **best** way to combine the ideas in sentences 29, 30, 31, and 32 into one sentence.

U.S. Navy Admiral Richard Byrd flew across the North Pole in 1926. He didn't see any holes. Then, he flew across the South Pole in 1929. He didn't see any holes then either.

  a. In 1926 and 1929, U.S. Navy Admiral Richard Byrd flew across the North Pole and didn't see any holes.
  b. In 1929, U.S. Navy Admiral Richard Byrd flew across the South Pole, but in 1926, he flew across the North Pole and didn't see any holes.
  c. U.S. Navy Admiral Richard Byrd flew across the North Pole in 1926 and the South Pole in 1929 without seeing any holes.
  d. U.S. Navy Admiral Richard Byrd flew across both the North and South Poles in 1929 and 1926, and he didn't see any holes the first time and he didn't see any holes the second time either.

9. Choose the correct way to write the underlined part of sentence 13.

He raised money to make a expedition to the North Pole to explore the inner Earth, but he was unsuccessful.

  a. He raised money to makes a expedition
  b. He raised money to make an expedition
  c. He raised money to make a espedition
  d. No change is needed.

10. Choose the correct way to write the underlined part of sentence 1.

British astronomer Edmund Halley is usually mentioned in connection with the comet that was named after he, Halley's Comet.

  a. comet that was named after he, halley's Comet.
  b. comet that was names after he, Halley's Comet.
  c. comet that was named after him, Halley's Comet.
  d. No change is needed.

Ellie's seventh-grade biology class has been studying zoology. Her teacher asks the class to write reports on animals or topics relating to animals. Ellie chooses her topic, researches it, compiles an outline, and writes her rough draft. She needs your help editing and revising it.

Here is Ellie's rough draft. Read it and then answer questions 1–10.

(1) Imagine that your just sitting down to some eggs and bacon on a Sunday morning when a coyote wanders past the kitchen window. (2) This is becoming more common every year as humans and animals are forced to share the same living spaces. (3) In fact, people are finding themselves living right alongside all kinds of wild animals.

(4) This trend is no longer that unusual. (5) Wildlife experts say that the human population are expanding into areas where animals already live. (6) Plus, by cleaning up old parks and creating new ones, birds and animals are being drawn to areas where people live. (7) As human beings destroy wildlife's natural habitat, they will be forced to share living spaces. (8) We all have to adapt somehow.

(9) As it is, hundreds of thousands of whitetail deer currently live in suburban and urban areas. (10) The suburban coyote population is on the rise as well. (11) Coyotes have even learned to live in New York City's Central Park. (12) They survive on garbage, grubs, rodents, and pets. (13) A family in Greenwich Connecticut, was surprised to find that a family of foxes had built a den under their shed in the backyard. (14) The mother expected the foxes to be a nuesance and her first impulse was to drive them out. (15) However, after being advised to be tolerant, she learned that the red fox and her "kits," or babies, were also a source of education for her family. (16) She and her children loved to watch the kits play. (17) Once the babies had grown, the fox family abandoned their den.

(18) Often, a persons' fear will cause more trouble than it has to. (19) For example, if a bear or fox wanders onto someone's property the person may report to the authorities that the animal has come to attack. (20) In fact, the animal is probably just passing through. (21) If people protect themselves and their belongings—covering trash cans and supervising household pets, for instance.

(22) Not every human-animal interaction is necessarily good, however. (23) Recently, a mountain lion attacked a man and woman in a wilderness park outside of Los Angeles. (24) The man was killed and the woman was critically hurt. (25) Nevertheless, animal experts believe that such attacks are rare. (26) People must be careful, but wildlife will keep to themselves for the most part.

(27) One thing we know for sure is that animals have learned to adapt to new environments. (28) Therefore, when wildlife arrives in a suburban or urban setting, they will take advantage of sources of food and habitat. (29) By taking the proper precautions and using good judgment, while respecting the rights of wildlife, people can help facilitate a harmonious living arrangement.

1. Choose the correct way to write the underlined part of sentence 18.

   Often, a <u>persons' fear will cause more trouble than</u> it has to.

   a. persons' fear will cause most trouble than
   b. person's fear will cause more trouble than
   c. persons' fear will cause more trouble then
   d. No change is needed.

2. Ellie wants to change sentence 3 so that it is more specific.

   In fact, people are finding themselves living right alongside <u>all kinds of wild animals.</u>

   Choose the **best** way to rewrite the underlined part of this sentence.

   a. different animals.
   b. a variety of birds and animals.
   c. animals that come from many different places.
   d. deer, Canada geese, coyotes, foxes, bear, and moose.

3. Choose the correct way to write the underlined part of sentence 29.

   By taking the proper precautions <u>and using good judgment</u>, while respecting the rights of wildlife, people can help facilitate a harmonious living arrangement.

   a. and used good judgment
   b. and using good judjement
   c. and using well judgment
   d. No change is needed.

4. Choose the correct way to write the underlined part of sentence 13.

   <u>A family in Greenwich Connecticut,</u> was surprised to find that a family of foxes had built a den under their shed in the backyard.

   a. A family in, Greenwich Connecticut,
   b. A family in Greenwich, Connecticut,
   c. A family in greenwich connecticut,
   d. No change is needed.

5. Read sentence 26, which is poorly written.

    People must be careful, but wildlife will keep to themselves for the most part.

    Choose the **best** way to rewrite this sentence.

    a. Wildlife will usually keep to themselves, but people should always be careful.
    b. People must be careful of wildlife keeping to themselves.
    c. Wildlife, who are keeping to themselves, are looking out for people who are trying to be careful.
    d. People must be careful because wildlife will keep to themselves for the most part.

6. Choose the correct way to write the underlined part of sentence 5.

    Wildlife <u>experts say that the human population are expanding</u> into areas where animals already live.

    a. experts say that the humans population are expanding
    b. experts say, that the human population are expanding
    c. experts say that the human population is expanding
    d. No change is needed.

7. Which of these is **not** a complete sentence?

    a. Imagine that your just sitting down to some eggs and bacon on a Sunday morning when a coyote wanders past the kitchen window.
    b. They survive on garbage, grubs, rodents, and pets.
    c. If people protect themselves and their belongings—covering trash cans and supervising household pets, for instance.
    d. One thing we know for sure is that animals have learned to adapt to new environments.

8. Choose the correct way to write the underlined part of sentence 19.

    For example, if a bear or fox <u>wanders onto someone's property the person</u> may report to the authorities that the animal has come to attack.

    a. wanders onto someones' property the person
    b. wanders onto someone's property, the person
    c. wandering onto someone's property the person
    d. No change is needed.

9. Choose the correct way to write the underlined part of sentence 1.

    <u>Imagine that your just sitting down to some eggs</u> and bacon on a Sunday morning when a coyote wanders past the kitchen window.

    a. Imagine that your just sitting down to some egg's
    b. Imagine that you just sitting down to some eggs
    c. Imagine that you're just sitting down to some eggs
    d. No change is needed.

10. Choose the correct way to write the underlined part of sentence 14.

    The mother expected the foxes to <u>be a nuesance and her first impulse</u> was to drive them out.

    a. be a nuesance and she first impulse
    b. be a nuisance and her first impulse
    c. have been a nuesance and her first impulse
    d. No change is needed.

Heather's seventh-grade English class is studying poetry. Her teacher asks her to write a report on an important poet and his or her message. Heather reads the newspaper, does some brainstorming, and writes her first draft. She needs your help editing and revising it.

Here is Heather's rough draft. Read it and then answer questions 1–10.

(1) Poet Mattie Stepanek faced challenges and hardships throughout his life. (2) He was known as a "peacemaker and poet, and his poetry celebrates the power of peace in a difficult world. (3) Stepanek was born with a rare neuromuscular disorder, a form of muscular dystrophy. (4) His illness did not stop him from spreading his message of peace.

(5) Stepanek started writing poetry at the age of three. (6) He wrote to help him work through his feelings about his disease, which caused muscle weakness as well as difficulties with heart rate and breathing. (7) He survived with the help of a power wheelchair, ventilator, and supplemental oxygen. (8) Stepanek's mother Jeni developed a milder version of the disease after giving birth to her four children and the family lost two brothers and a sister to it.

(9) Stepanek was inspired to write about the power of love and peace. (10) When he appeared on the Oprah Winfrey Show, he told the audience that he expressed his thoughts and feelings through writing. (11) The audience was mostly women. (12) "You're heartsong is your inner beauty," said Stepanek. (13) "it's the song in your heart that wants you to help make yourself a better person, and to help other people do the same. (14) Everybody has one." (15) This loving message helped to turn his five published poetry books into bestsellers. (16) They include *Heartsongs*, *Hope Through Heartsongs*, and *Celebrate Through Heartsongs*.

(17) Stepanek had the honor of meeting and establishing a friendship with the former president, Jimmy Carter, who is also an advocate for peace. (18) Him and Carter may even have been working on a book about peacemaking together. (19) Before the war in Iraq began, Stepanek sent a poem to president George W. Bush, asking him to seek peace. (20) "We cannot get caught with a bad attitude or we are not choosing peace," it read in part.

(21) Stepanek served as the National Goodwill Ambassador for the Muscular Dystrophy Association. (22) He also excelled in his educational pursuits and earned a junior black belt in martial arts. (23) He once said, "I want people to know my life philosophy, to remember to play after every storm."

(24) Mattie Stepanek died on June 22 2004, in Washington, D.C. (25) Nonetheless, muscular dystrophy could never silence his message of peace and love. (26) It's too bad he had to die because he was such a brave, honest, and gifted poet. (27) July 14, 2004, would have been his fourteenth birthday.

1. Read sentence 8, which is poorly written.

   Stepanek's mother Jeni developed a milder version of the disease after giving birth to her four children and the family lost two brothers and a sister to it.

   Choose the **best** way to rewrite this sentence.

   a. Stepanek's mother developed a milder version of the disease, after giving birth to her four children, Jeni, two brothers, and a sister.
   b. Stepanek's mother Jeni, developed a milder version of the disease, after giving birth to her four childrren, and the family, lost two brothers, and a sister to it.
   c. Stepanek's mother, Jeni, developed a milder version of the disease after giving birth to her four children, and the family lost two brothers and a sister to it.
   d. Stepanek developed a milder version of the disease from his mother, Jeni, who then gave it to her two brothers and a sister.

2. Choose the correct way to write the underlined part of sentence 13.

   "it's the song in your heart that wants you to help make yourself a better person, and to help other people do the same.

   a. "its the song in your heart
   b. "it's the song in you heart
   c. "It's the song in your heart
   d. No change is needed.

3. Choose the word or phrase that **best** fits at the beginning of sentence 4.

   a. For example,
   b. Nonetheless,
   c. Then,
   d. Sadly,

4. Choose the correct way to write the underlined part of sentence 18.

   Him and Carter may even have been working on a book about peacemaking together.

   a. He and Carter may even have been working
   b. Him and Carter may even having been working
   c. Him and carter may even have been working
   d. No change is needed.

5. Choose the correct way to write the underlined part of sentence 19.

   Before the war in Iraq began, Stepanek sent a poem to **president George W. Bush, asking him** to seek peace.

   a. president George W. Bush asking him
   b. president George W. Bush, asking he
   c. President George W. Bush, asking him
   d. No change is needed.

6. Choose the sentence that does **not** belong in the paragraph that begins with sentence 9.

   a. sentence 9
   b. sentence 10
   c. sentence 11
   d. sentence 15

7. Choose the correct way to write the underlined part of sentence 2.

   He was known as a **"peacemaker and poet, and his poetry celebrates** the power of peace in a difficult world.

   a. "peacemaker and poet," and his poetry celebrates
   b. "peacemaker and poet, and his poetry cellebrates
   c. "peacemaker and poet, and him poetry celebrates
   d. No change is needed.

8. Choose the **best** way to write the underlined part of sentence 26 so that the composition maintains a consistent tone.

   <u>It's too bad he had to die because</u> he was such a brave, honest, and gifted poet.

   a. He had a good message to spread, cause
   b. Our country is lucky to have known him, even for a short while, because
   c. He died without having spread his message very far, even though
   d. It's awful that he had to die, since

9. Choose the correct way to write the underlined part of sentence 12.

   <u>"You're heartsong is your inner beauty,"</u> said Stepanek.

   a. "You're heartsong is you're inner beauty,"
   b. "Your heartsong is your inner beauty,"
   c. "You're heartsong is your inner beauty"
   d. No change is needed.

10. Choose the correct way to write the underlined part of sentence 24.

    Mattie Stepanek died on <u>June 22 2004, in Washington, D.C.</u>

    a. June 22 2004, in Washington, d.c.
    b. June 22 2004, in Washington D.C.
    c. June 22, 2004, in Washington, D.C.
    d. No change is needed.

72

Noah has been asked by his seventh-grade English teacher to write a persuasive report on a subject relating to summer vacations. Noah brainstorms some of his ideas and draws up an outline. He has written his rough draft, but needs your help editing and revising it.

Here is Noah's rough draft. Read it and then answer questions 1–10.

(1) When you're out looking for summer fun this season, try something a little different. (2) The popular national parks like yosemite, Old Faithful, and Grand Canyon aren't all there are to see. (3) In fact, the National Park Service manages 388 national parks, seashores, monuments, and historic sites. (4) Get out there and explore them?

(5) Dinosaur National Monument in Colorado is wonderful. (6) It includes a "Dinosaur Quarry," where visitors can see fossils and bones, as well as caves with rock art. (7) Not interested in giant extinct lizards? (8) You can also go camping, hiking biking, or whitewater rafting down the Yampa and Green Rivers.

(9) If you're looking for something along the coast, Biscayne National Park in Florida is an 175,000-acre oasis. (10) It features water and living coral reefs. (11) In Georgia, Cumberland Island National Seashore offers sparkling beaches and dunes, maritime forests, salt marshes, and freshwater lakes. (12) Hike along the public paths or visit the former vacation homes of the famous Carnegie and Rockefeller families. (13) Sleeping Bear Dunes National Lakeshore in Michigan was a U.S. Coast Guard rescue station during World War II. (14) If you visit today, you can watch reenactments of rescue crews saving shipwreck victims. (15) That's not all.

(16) State parks offer another option this summer. (17) I live in the state of Nevada. (18) The "Grand Canyon of the East," for example, is Letchworth State Park in New York. (19) Here you can find the Genesee River flowing amid six-hundred-foot-high cliffs. (20) Wisconsin's Copper Falls State Park features ancient lava flows, deep gorges, and spectacular waterfalls.

(21) Not even rainy weather can stop you this year. (22) Rainy-day activities are there for entertainment. (23) Get involved in audio-visual programs, archeological exhibits, museums, guided and self-guided tours, and demonstrations. (24) Another alternative is to pack rainy-day gear so you can experience the park in wet weather. (25) (All kids like playing in the mud.)

(26) Why would you want to explore something new? (27) These parks are perfect for families with small children because there less crowded and less stressful for parents. (28) Plus, they're often more affordable in terms of camping fees and entrance fees. (29) You should know that some small parks do not have all the things large parks do. (30) Some of the smaller parks may not offer flushing toilets, cold running water, or facilities for RVs. (31) Call ahead to be sure.

(32) Families can find these little known parks by visiting the National Park Service website (www.nps.gov). (33) Make an effort this summer to find a new "favorite vacation spot.

1. Read sentence 22, which is poorly written.

   Rainy-day activities are there for entertainment.

   Choose the **best** way to rewrite this sentence.

   a. Rainy-day activities are entertaining there.
   b. Entertaining activities, such as rainy-day activities, are there for your entertainment.
   c. There are rainy-day activities at many parks, which are entertaining.
   d. Rainy-day activities are planned to keep you and your family entertained.

2. Choose the correct way to write the underlined part of sentence 4.

   Get out there and <u>explore them?</u>

   a. explore them!
   b. explore there?
   c. explores them?
   d. No change is needed.

3. Choose the correct way to write the underlined part of sentence 8.

   You can also go <u>camping, hiking biking, or whitewater rafting down the Yampa and Green Rivers.</u>

   a. camping, hiking biking, or whitewater rafting down the Yampa and Green rivers.
   b. camping, hiking, biking, or whitewater rafting down the Yampa and Green Rivers.
   c. camping, hiking biking, or whitewater rafting down the Yampa, and Green Rivers.
   d. No change is needed.

4. Choose the sentence that does **not** belong in the paragraph that begins with sentence 16.

   a. sentence 16
   b. sentence 17
   c. sentence 19
   d. sentence 20

74

5. Choose the correct way to write the underlined part of sentence 9.

   If you're looking for something along the coast, Biscayne National Park in Florida is an 175,000-acre oasis.

   a. Florida is the 175,000-acre oasis.
   b. Florida is a 175,000-acre oasis.
   c. Florida, is an 175,000-acre oasis.
   d. No change is needed.

6. Choose the sentence that could **best** be added right after sentence 15.

   a. The U.S. Coast Guard is helpful across the nation.
   b. There's more than just reenactments at Sleeping Bear Dunes National Lakeshore.
   c. Visitors can also swim, snorkel, scuba dive, fish, hike, kayak, and camp.
   d. This park is in Michigan.

7. Choose the correct way to write the underlined part of sentence 2.

   The popular national parks like yosemite, Old Faithful, and Grand Canyon aren't all there are to see.

   a. like Yosemite, Old Faithful, and Grand Canyon aren't all there are to see.
   b. like yosemite, Old Faithful, and Grand Canyon isn't all there are to see.
   c. like yosemite, Old Faithful, and Grand Canyon aren't all they're are to see.
   d. No change is needed.

8. Choose the correct way to write the underlined part of sentence 33.

   Make an effort this summer to find a new "favorite vacation spot.

   a. to find a new "favorite vacation spot."
   b. two find a new "favorite vacation spot.
   c. to find a new, "favorite vacation spot.
   d. No change is needed.

9. Choose the correct way to write the underlined part of sentence 27.

    These parks are perfect for families <u>with small children because there less crowded</u> and less stressful for parents.

    a. with small child because there less crowded
    b. with small children, because there less crowded
    c. with small children because they're less crowded
    d. No change is needed.

10. Choose the **best** way to combine the ideas in sentences 29 and 30 into one sentence.

    You should know that some small parks do not have all the things large parks do. Some of the smaller parks may not offer flushing toilets, cold running water, or facilities for RVs.

    a. All small parks are missing some of the things that large parks have, such as flushing toilets, cold running water, or facilities for RVs.
    b. Flushing toilets, cold running water, or facilities for RVs can be found in small parks, but only when there aren't any large parks nearby that have flushing toilets, cold running water, or facilities for RVs.
    c. Large parks do have flushing toilets, cold running water, or facilities for RVs, but small parks don't have those things.
    d. You should be aware, however, that some of the smaller parks may not offer flushing toilets, cold running water, or facilities for RVs.

Florence's seventh-grade social studies class is studying Latin American countries. Her teacher has asked each student to pretend he or she is from one of those countries and to write an imaginative story describing the culture. Florence chooses Paraguay, develops an outline, and writes her rough draft. She needs your help editing and revising it.

Here is Florence's rough draft. Read it and then answer questions 1–10.

(1) Similar to the United States, outside groups helped to expand Paraguayan culture. (2) Spanish, Italians, Germans, Russians, Jews, Poles, Ukrainians, Mennonites, Australians, Japanese, and small native tribes all contributed. (3) Over time, the groups became part of the country as a whole. (4) Today, Paraguay is a diverse and multicultural nation. (5) It is the only officially bilinngaul country in Latin America. (6) Besides Spanish, close to ninety percent of the population speaks Guarani.

(7) Folklore makes up the spiritual portion of the Paraguayan culture. (8) Paraguayan folklore is a combination of that of Hispanic cultures and smaller native tribes. (9) Music, dance, dresses, and food traditions are all tied to the country's folklore. (10) When visiting Paraguay, one may see religious festivals, fairs, and charity bazaars, which are all part of the people's folklore traditions.

(11) Music is very essential to Paraguayan customs. (12) The polka appeared around 1856. (13) It is very different from European polkas. (14) The Paraguayan polka is a happy, rhythmic sound adopted from Spanish music. (15) Jose Asuncion Flores created *guarania* in 1925. (16) This musical form emphasizes melody which makes it more for listening than for dancing.

(17) Paraguay's artisans are involved in many different skills and trades. (18) Weavers produce some of the finest silk, called *ñanduti* (or spider web silk). (19) *Ñanduti* came from the Canary Islands in Spain. (20) It is often crafted into floral designs. (21) Other artisans weave wool, make cotton bedspreads, and craft ponchos. (22) Some work in leather, silver, and gold. (23) Many craftsmen make baskets. (24) The most famous *santeros* are craftsmen who make religious images and objects. (25) They mostly carve wood into masks, crafts, and musical instruments.

(26) Paraguay's cuisine shows the countrys multicultural roots. (27) Their food varies from homemade country food, always served with *chipas* (wheat rolls prepared with manioc and cheese). (28) To river fish and meat. (29) Paraguayan food is one of the country's most popular attractions.

(30) Paraguayan sports are an important aspect of the country's culture as well. (31) They enjoy basketball, soccer, and other group sports. (32) Soccer is the most popular sport. (33) The Paraguayan Soccer League was formed in 1906. (34) Paraguay qualified for the World Cups in Sweden in 1958, Mexico in 1986 France in 1998, and Korea in 2001.

(35) Paraguay's multicultural identity influences all aspects of its traditions and customs. (36) The Paraguay of today were an ever-evolving gathering of the many cultures that have chosen to settle there.

1. Choose the correct way to write the underlined part of sentence 26.

    Paraguay's <u>cuisine shows the countrys</u> multicultural roots.

    a. cuisine show the countrys
    b. cuisine shows the country's
    c. quisine shows the countrys
    d. No change is needed.

2. Choose the correct way to write the underlined part of sentence 10.

    <u>When visiting Paraguay, one may see</u> religious festivals, fairs, and charity bazaars, which are all part of the people's folklore traditions.

    a. When visiting paraguay, one may see
    b. When visiting Paraguay, won may see
    c. When visited Paraguay, one may see
    d. No change is needed.

3. Florence wants to add this sentence to the paragraph that begins with sentence 1.

    Each of these diverse groups started out in a colony or a small settlement where it maintained its own customs.

    Where would the sentence **best** fit?

    a. right after sentence 1
    b. right after sentence 2
    c. right after sentence 4
    d. right after sentence 5

4. Choose the correct way to write the underlined part of sentence 36.

   The Paraguay of today <u>were an ever-evolving gathering</u> of the many cultures that have chosen to settle there.

   a. were an ever-evolving gathered
   b. is an ever-evolving gathering
   c. were an ever-evolving, gathering
   d. No change is needed.

5. The topic sentence of the paragraph that begins with sentence 7 is

   a. sentence 7.
   b. sentence 8.
   c. sentence 9.
   d. sentence 10.

6. Choose the correct way to write the underlined part of sentence 34.

   Paraguay qualified for the World Cups in <u>Sweden in 1958, Mexico in 1986 France in 1998, and Korea in 2001.</u>

   a. Sweden in 1958, Mexico in 1986, France in 1998, and Korea in 2001.
   b. Sweden in 1958 Mexico in 1986 France in 1998 and Korea in 2001.
   c. Sweden on 1958, Mexico on 1986 France on 1998, and Korea on 2001.
   d. No change is needed.

7. Which of these is **not** a complete sentence?

   a. It is very different from European polkas.
   b. It is often crafted into floral designs.
   c. To river fish and meat.
   d. Soccer is the most popular sport.

8. Choose the correct way to write the underlined part of sentence 5.

   It is the only officially <u>bilinngaul country in Latin America.</u>

   a. bilingual country in Latin America.
   b. bilinngaul country in latin america.
   c. bilinngaul country, in Latin America.
   d. No change is needed.

9. Choose the correct way to write the underlined part of sentence 16.

   This musical form <u>emphasizes melody which makes</u> it more for listening than for dancing.

   a. emphasizes melody which make
   b. emphasizes melody, which makes
   c. imphasizes melody which makes
   d. No change is needed.

10. Florence wants to change sentence 11 so that it is more specific.

   Music is very essential to Paraguayan customs.

   Choose the **best** way to rewrite this sentence.

   a. Paraguayan customs need music.
   b. Music is one of the most essential aspects of Paraguay's cultural identity.
   c. Paraguay and music are essential to Paraguayan culture.
   d. Music is an essential part of Paraguayan customs.

In her studies of ancient Greece, Mary found an interesting sidebar about Greek female slaves in her history textbook. When her seventh-grade history teacher asked the class to write a report on a topic pertaining to ancient Greece, Mary eagerly began writing her rough draft. She needs your help editing and revising it.

Here is Mary's rough draft. Read it and then answer questions 1–10.

(1) While a lot of information exists about Greek men's political military and cultural achievements we know little of the role of women in ancient Greece. (2) What we do know comes from plays, philosophical texts, vase paintings, and sculptures (all created by males). (3) Even the upper-class women were treated, by today's standards, as little more than slaves. (4) We can only imagine how life for actual slave women (*thmoïs*) must have been due to they're gender and social status.

(5) Athenian women were broken down into three classes. (6) The most low class included the slave women. (7) The second class was that of the Athenian citizen women, who were the wives of the men in Greek society. (8) The third class was known as the "hetaerae." (9) The hetaerae were given an education in reading, writing, and music. (10) They were allowed into the Agora and other places that were off-limits to citizen and slave women. (11) (For the most part, however, sources show that the hetaerae were no better then ancient prostitutes.)

(12) Slavery was common in the ancient world. (13) Only in the poorest households were wives expected to do all the chores. (14) These women also had to work in the fields or in stalls in the marketplace alongside men. (15) Female slaves were usually the result of the spoils of a foreign war. (16) It is unknown how much they cost. (17) A document from 415 B.C.E. shows that the price of female slaves ranged from 220 drachmas to 85 drachmas. (18) They were given many domestic tasks, such as shopping, getting wood, cooking and serving food, cleaning caring for children, and weaving wool. (19) In wealthier households, some female slaves also worked as housekeepers, cooks, and nurses.

(20) An owner's personality and the slave's status determined how the slave was treated in the household. (21) A female slave was often sexually and physically abused. (22) Since female slaves were not allowed to raise their own children, any children born from a relationship between a slave and her master were done away with. (23) Slaves could not even marry, since marriage were seen as a special privilege of the Athens elite.

(24) Although not required of them, slave girls often developed personal relationships with their mistresses. (25) Upper-class women were kept isolated in their homes. (26) They often turned to their slave girls for companionship. (27) Female slaves went with their mistresses on outings as well. (28) Tombstones with scenes of familiarity between a woman and her slave further display this bond. (29) Both upper-class and slave women most likely drew closer together because of their exclusion from Athenian society.

(continued on next page)

81

(continued from previous page)

> (30) All women were allowed to participate in religion. (31) In fact, religion was the only public event all women could take part in. (32) Slave women were included in some religious affairs and could be initiated into the Eleusinian Mysteries, which celebrated the myth of persephone.
>
> (33) Slavery was an important part of ancient Greek life. (34) While an unfortunate truth, perhaps the bonds women were able to form across social-class lines helped to justify the struggle.

1. Choose the correct way to write the underlined part of sentence 32.

   Slave women were included in some religious affairs and could be initiated into the Eleusinian Mysteries, <u>which celebrated the myth of persephone.</u>

   a. which celebrated the myth, of persephone.
   b. which celebrated the mith of persephone.
   c. which celebrated the myth of Persephone.
   d. No change is needed.

2. Read sentence 1, which is poorly written.

   While a lot of information exists about Greek men's political military and cultural achievements we know little of the role of women in ancient Greece.

   Choose the **best** way to rewrite this sentence.

   a. While a lot of information exists about Greek mens' political military and cultural achievements we know lesser of the role of the womens' in ancient Greece.
   b. Information about Greek men's political, military, and cultural achievements is plentiful, while we know a lot less information of the role of women in ancient Greece.
   c. While much information exists about Greek men's political, military, and cultural achievements, we know little of the role women played in ancient Greece.
   d. Women and men in ancient Greece were political, military, and cultural, but we have little information on the role of women in ancient Greece.

3. Choose the correct way to write the underlined part of sentence 23.

Slaves could not even marry, <u>since marriage were seen</u> as a special privilege of the Athens elite.

   a. since marriage was seen
   b. since marryage were seen
   c. since marriage were scene
   d. No change is needed.

4. Choose the correct way to write the underlined part of sentence 6.

<u>The most low class</u> included the slave women.

   a. The most low classes
   b. The lowest class
   c. The more low class
   d. No change is needed.

5. Read sentence 29, which is poorly written.

Both upper-class and slave women most likely drew closer together because of their exclusion from Athenian society.

Choose the **best** way to rewrite this sentence.

   a. Upper-class and slave women were probably drawn closer together because they were both excluded from Athenian society.
   b. Upper-class and slave women, both excluded from Athenian society, were drawn closer together most likely because they were excluded.
   c. Athenian society excluded upper-class and slave women, but that meant they were drawn closer together to Athenian society.
   d. They were both excluded, upper-class and slaves, but they were closer together, too.

6. Choose the word or phrase that **best** fits at the beginning of sentence 22.

    a. For example,
    b. Then,
    c. Fortunately,
    d. However,

7. Choose the correct way to write the underlined part of sentence 11.

(For the most part, however, sources show that the hetaerae were <u>no better then ancient prostitutes.</u>)

    a. no better then ancient prostitutes.
    b. no better than ancient prostitutes.)
    c. no better then ancient, prostitutes.)
    d. No change is needed.

8. Choose the **best** way to combine the ideas in sentences 30 and 31 into one sentence.

All women were allowed to participate in religion. In fact, religion was the only public event all women could take part in.

    a. Women could take part and participate in religion, but it was the only public event they could take part in.
    b. Religion was a public event. It was the only public event women could participate in.
    c. Women were allowed to publicly participate in religion, and that was the only thing they could do publicly.
    d. Religion was the only public event in which all women were allowed to participate.

9. Choose the correct way to write the underlined part of sentence 4.

   We can only imagine how life for actual slave women (*thmoïs*) must have been <u>due to they're gender and social status.</u>

   a. due to their gender and social status.
   b. due to they're gender and social statuses.
   c. due too they're gender and social status.
   d. No change is needed.

10. Choose the correct way to write the underlined part of sentence 18.

   They were given many domestic tasks, such as shopping, getting wood, cooking <u>and serving food, cleaning caring for children, and weaving wool.</u>

   a. and serving food cleaning caring for children and weaving wool.
   b. and serving food, cleaning caring for children, and, weaving wool.
   c. and serving food, cleaning, caring for children, and weaving wool.
   d. No change is needed.

Polly's seventh-grade English class has been working on their creative writing skills. Their teacher told them each to write a story that included setting, plot, characters, and details. Polly made a web of ideas and wrote her rough draft. She needs your help editing and revising the beginning of it.

Here is Polly's rough draft. Read it and then answer questions 1–10.

(1) I'd been living in this little town called Burgsberg. (2) It wasn't too far from anything you might need, but it wasn't two close to anything either. (3) I was sitting on the front porch, taking stock of my apple orchards and smiling on the livestock. (4) I had been expecting a visit from the two men I most respect on this earth, Joe Frank and Mr. Eddie West.

(5) Now Joe Frank didn't expect a "Mr." at the front of his name since he had divorced the former Mrs. Joe Frank and liked to keep it that way. (6) He enjoyed the bachelor's life and so we didn't burden him with all the business of being called "Mr." (7) He worked down at the mine as a foreman. (8) He could fool you into thinking that someone had outlined all the veins with a black pen under his skin because his skin creases were so thickened with soot and his skin was so rough. (9) We all figured his divorce was the result of Mrs. Joe Frank being tired of washing soot out of she white bed sheets, but no one had the courage to ask Joe if that was the case.

(10) Mr. Eddie West, on the other hand, knew his business of being both a married man and a man about the town. (11) He worked in loans and securities at the National Bank of Burgsberg. (12) He could hold his own like any respectable village man. (13) He didn't like to brag about the fact that he had once taken down two young men in the next town over. (14) The boys had had fancy ideas about stealing Eddie's car. (15) Now one boy wishes he could go back to walking without a limp. (16) The other boy dreams about the day when hair will grow back over the bald spot Eddie gave him. (17) That Mr. Eddie West always was a tough guy.

(18) As I said, I had been expecting these respectable men for a little under a half hour. (19) It was getting on toward dinnertime and I could smell the pork chops frying on the stovetop. (20) A warm breeze was lying on the tall, untrimmed grasses alongside the porch. (21) Even they seemed to know that the day was done.

(22) The sound of an engine grew steadily louder and Joe Frank's 1963 chevrolet Belair made its way up the driveway. (23) My wife, Kristine, was calling me from inside, but I knew that what Eddie, Joe, and I had to talk about was far more important than any supper plate. (24) I rose from the porch steps and met Joe at his driver's side door. (25) "Hello, Joe, I said, shaking his hand. (26) "Eddie, how've you been?"

(27) "Oh, I'm just fine, Dom," Eddie replied, climbing out from the other side of the car. (28) "What's this I hear about a proposition? (29) The last time you came up with one of your brilliant ideas, we all ended up in jail and I nearly lost my job at the bank."

(continued on next page)

(continued from previous page)

(30) "Yeah, Dom," Joe said. (31) "What's it about this time."

(32) "This is pure, inspired genius this time, gentlemen," I assured them proudly. (33) "I thought of something last night and I've been waiting all day to tell you about it." (34) I know for a fact that, for all that they are respectable, Joe and Eddie may be the least patient men in Burgsberg or anywhere else. (35) I looked from one sober face to the other, biding my time while hoping to pique their interests.

(36) "You make me wait any longer, Dom, and I'll get right back in that car there," Eddie said as he turned to face Joe. (37) "And you'll drive me home, Joe. (38) Dom's news can't be worth the spit its settling on."

(39) "All right," I hastily said, not wanting to lose their attention. (40) "Gentlemen, I beleive I have come up with a way to . . . ," I began, allowing myself just one more tiny dramatic pause before I continued, "to travel through time."

1. Choose the correct way to write the underlined part of sentence 38.

   Dom's news can't <u>be worth the spit its settling</u> on."

   a. be worth the spit its settleing
   b. be worth the spit it's settling
   c. been worth the spit its settling
   d. No change is needed.

2. Choose the **best** way to combine the ideas in sentences 15 and 16 into one sentence.

   Now one boy wishes he could go back to walking without a limp. The other boy dreams about the day when hair will grow back over the bald spot Eddie gave him.

   a. Now one boy wishes he could go back to walking without a limp, while the other boy dreams of the day when hair will grow back over the bald spot Eddie gave him.
   b. Now one boy goes back to walking with a limp and the other boy dreams about the day when hair will grow back over the bald spot Eddie gave him.
   c. Now one boy and the other boy dream of walking without a limp and about the day when hair will grow back over the bald spot Eddie gave him.
   d. Now one boy walks with a limp and the other boy has a bald spot.

3. Choose the correct way to write the underlined part of sentence 9.

   We all figured his divorce was the result of <u>Mrs. Joe Frank being tired of washing soot out of she white bed sheets,</u> but no one had the courage to ask Joe if that was the case.

   a. Mrs. Joe Frank was tired of washing soot out of she white bed sheets,
   b. Mrs. Joe Frank, being tired of washing soot out of she white bed sheets,
   c. Mrs. Joe Frank being tired of washing soot out of her white bed sheets,
   d. No change is needed.

4. Polly wants to add this sentence to the paragraph that begins with sentence 32.

   All the same, I wanted to give my news the proper weight by not blurting it out right away.

   Where would the sentence **best** fit?

   a. right after sentence 32
   b. right after sentence 33
   c. right after sentence 34
   d. right after sentence 35

5. Choose the correct way to write the underlined part of sentence 25.

   "Hello, <u>Joe, I said, shaking his hand.</u>

   a. Joe, I said, shaking him hand.
   b. Joe," I said, shaking his hand.
   c. Joe, i said, shaking his hand.
   d. No change is needed.

6. Choose the correct way to write the underlined part of sentence 2.

It wasn't too far from anything you might need, but <u>it wasn't two close to anything either.</u>

    a.   it wasn't too close to anything either.
    b.   it wasn't two close to, anything either.
    c.   it wasn't two close to anything either?
    d.   No change is needed.

7. Read sentence 8, which is poorly written.

He could fool you into thinking that someone had outlined all the veins with a black pen under his skin because his skin creases were so thickened with soot and his skin was so rough.

Choose the **best** way to rewrite this sentence.

    a.   His skin was rough, thickened by soot, and outlined with black pen under his veins, which he could fool you into thinking.
    b.   He could fool you into thinking his rough skin was thickened with soot when in actuality it was outlined with black pen.
    c.   Black pen and soot thickened his rough skin, all in the creases, but he couldn't fool you.
    d.   The creases of his rough skin were so thickened with soot that he could fool you into thinking that someone had outlined all his veins in black pen.

8. Choose the correct way to write the underlined part of sentence 40.

<u>"Gentlemen, I beleive I have come up with</u> a way to . . . ," I began, allowing myself just one more tiny dramatic pause before I continued, "to travel through time."

    a.   "Gentlemen," I beleive I have come up with
    b.   "Gentlemen, I believe I have come up with
    c.   "Gentlemen, I beleive I had come up with
    d.   No change is needed.

9. Choose the correct way to write the underlined part of sentence 31.

"What's <u>it about this time.</u>"

    a. it about this time?"
    b. it, about this time."
    c. it about these time."
    d. No change is needed.

10. Choose the correct way to write the underlined part of sentence 22.

The sound of an engine grew steadily louder and Joe Frank's <u>1963 chevrolet Belair made its way up the driveway.</u>

    a. 1963 chevrolet Belair make its way up the driveway.
    b. 1963 chevrolet Belair made it's way up the driveway.
    c. 1963 Chevrolet Belair made its way up the driveway.
    d. No change is needed.

Zeke's seventh-grade biology class has been studying physiological processes. His teacher asks each student to write a report on one of the body's processes. Zeke visits the school library and writes his rough draft. He needs your help editing and revising it.

Here is Zeke's rough draft. Read it and then answer questions 1–10.

(1) It is interesting that as it grows darker in the evening, we generally seem to get more tired. (2) Perhaps you've noticed that you have more energy at a certain point in the day. (3) A process, called a "circadian rhythm," is going on within we. (4) The term, circadian, comes from two Latin words: *circa*, meaning "about," and *dies*, meaning "day." (5) You may have heard it referred to as a "body clock."

(6) Within the hypothalamus in our brains is a trigger that tells us that it is time for sleep. (7) A gland called the pineal gland is regulated by light that comes in through our eyes. (8) When there is less light, a hormone called melatonin is produced. (9) When it gets darker outside, melatonin levels increase in our bodies. (10) A signal is then sent to our hypothalamus and we get sleepy. (11) When there is more light coming in through our eyes, melatonin production decreases. (12) When our eyes receive light, as in the morning, our body clock resets itself. (13) This entire process is a circadian rhythm.

(14) Other elements of our daily routines also act to reset our body clocks. (15) Physical activity temperature, and social routines often play a part. (16) Light and darkness are the only factors that seem to consistently affect the rhythm of our bodies. (17) In experiments, the circadian rhythms of animals kept in total darkness for extended periods of time became highly irregular.

(18) Many problems can arise if your body clock malfunctions. (19) If you have ever experienced "jet lag" you know how it feels when your sleep/awake cycle is interrupted. (20) Fatigue, disorientation, and insomnia are all associated with these kinds of interruptions. (21) A disorder called "advanced sleep phase syndrome" causes a person to feel listless in the evening, while sleeping longer in the morning. (22) Blind people often suffer from "hypernychthemeral syndrome." (23) They will stay up later and later every night and wake up later every morning after staying up late every night.

(24) The most common disorder is "delayed sleep phase syndrome," or DSPS. (25) Some people who have DSPS think that they are night owls because they notice that their minds work best at a later time than most people's and most of them fall asleep later than normal, sometimes not until early morning. (26) Since they usually fall asleep at the same time every night, people with DSPS are actually on a schedule. (27) Problems will arise when they have to woke up early in the morning. (28) Until 1981, when DSPS was classified as a sleeping disorder, sufferers were just thought to be lazy.

(29) Keeping your circadian rhythm intact is essential to being healthy. (30) Avoid the short-term negative affects of disrupting your sleep schedule and you will enjoy a better, restfuller lifestyle.

1. The topic sentence of the paragraph that begins with sentence 18 is

    a. sentence 18.
    b. sentence 20.
    c. sentence 21.
    d. sentence 23.

2. Read sentence 23, which is poorly written.

    They will stay up later and later every night and wake up later every morning after staying up late every night.

    Choose the **best** way to rewrite this sentence.

    a. They will wake up later every morning, stay up later and later every night.
    b. They will stay up later and later, wake up later and later, stay up later and later.
    c. They will stay up later and later every night and wake up later every morning.
    d. They will wake up later after having stayed up later and later and later.

3. Choose the correct way to write the underlined part of sentence 3.

    A process, called a "circadian rhythm," <u>is going on within we.</u>

    a. are going on within we.
    b. is going on within us.
    c. is gone on within we.
    d. No change is needed.

4. Choose the correct way to write the underlined part of sentence 27.

    Problems <u>will arise when they have to woke</u> up early in the morning.

    a. would arise when they have to woke
    b. will arise when they have to wake
    c. will arise when they have two woke
    d. No change is needed.

5. Choose the correct way to write the underlined part of sentence 15.

   <u>Physical activity temperature, and</u> social routines often play a part.

   a. Physical activity, temperature, and
   b. Physical, activity temperature, and
   c. Physical activity temperature and
   d. No change is needed.

6. Read sentence 25, which is poorly written.

   Some people who have DSPS think that they are night owls because they notice that their minds work best at a later time than most people's and most of them fall asleep later than normal, sometimes not until early morning.

   Choose the **best** way to rewrite this sentence.

   a. Some people who have DSPS may think they work best at a later time like night owls, but then they fall asleep later than normal, sometimes not until early morning.
   b. Some DSPS people are night owls who work best at a later time than most, but they also fall asleep in the early morning.
   c. Some people fall asleep in the early morning, while others fall asleep later than normal. They all have DSPS like most people.
   d. Some people who have DSPS may think that they are night owls. Their minds work best at a later time than most people's. Most sufferers fall asleep later than normal, sometimes not until early morning.

7. Choose the correct way to write the underlined part of sentence 19.

   If you have ever <u>experienced "jet lag" you know how it feels when your</u> sleep/awake cycle is interrupted.

   a. experienced "jet lag" you know how it felt when your
   b. experienced "jet lag," you know how it feels when your
   c. experienced "jet lag" you know how it feels when you're
   d. No change is needed.

8. Choose the correct way to write the underlined part of sentence 29.

<u>Keeping your circadian rhythm intact</u> is essential to being healthy.

    a. Keeping you're circadian rhythm intact
    b. Keeping your circadian rhythm entact
    c. Keeping your circadian rhythm, intact
    d. No change is needed.

9. Choose the correct way to write the underlined part of sentence 30.

Avoid the short-term negative affects of disrupting your sleep schedule and <u>you will enjoy a better, restfuller lifestyle.</u>

    a. you will enjoy a better, more restful lifestyle.
    b. you will enjoy a better, restfuller lifestyle!
    c. you will enjoy a better restfuller lifestyle.
    d. No change is needed.

10. Choose the word or phrase that **best** fits at the beginning of sentence 9.

    a. For example,
    b. Now,
    c. Therefore,
    d. First,

Gerry's seventh-grade history class is studying civil rights. His teacher asks the class to write biographies on men and women involved in civil rights in the twentieth century. Gerry chooses Medgar Evers, does some research, and writes his rough draft. He needs your help editing and revising it.

Here is Gerry's rough draft. Read it and then answer questions 1–10.

(1) Medgar Wiley Evers was born on July 2 1925, near Decatur, Mississippi. (2) He was drafted into the army during World War II. (3) When he returned home, he found that he still couldn't drink from the same water fountains, eat at the same lunch counters, or ride the same trains as white people. (4) Evers's battle for civil rights had begun.

(5) In 1946, at Decatur's courthouse, Evers was turned away from trying to register to vote. (6) From 1954 to 1963, he served as field secretary for Mississippi in the NAACP. (7) He traveled throughout his home state, encouraging African Americans to register to vote. (8) He also fought for integrated schools and organized boycotts against white-owned firms that practiced racial discrimmanation.

(9) Although he faced daily hardship, Evers couldn't imagine leaving the southern states. (10) In a magazine article written in 1954, Evers said of the south, "I don't choose to live anywhere else. (11) There's land here, where a man can raise cattle, and I'm going to do it some day."

(12) It didn't take long for Evers to become a target for racists. (13) On June 12, 1963, Evers was shot and killed outside his home in Jackson Mississippi. (14) Ten days later, police arrested white supremacist Byron De La Beckwith for the murder. (15) Two all-white juries could not reach a verdict on the case. (16) In 1969, the charges against Beckwith were dropped. (17) Twenty years later, the case was reopened with new charges. (18) In 1994, a jury of eight African Americans and four whites convicted Beckwith of Evers's murder.

(19) Demonstrators in the black community marched after Evers's funeral procession, shouting, "After Medgar, no more fear! (20) Local resident Walter Gardner said that this event made him realize the importance of acting for what you believe in. (21) Doing "something to be a participant and not a bystander in our society."

(22) In 1969, Evers's brother, Charles, became the first African-American mayor to be elected in Mississippi. (23) In an interview with national public radio, Charles said, "Medgar and I said many years ago, if we ever end the violent racism in this state, it'll be the greatest state in the world to live. (24) And now, Medgar, I know your gone, but I'm telling you, son, it's come to pass."

(25) Evers did a lot of stuff for African Americans. (26) His legacy lived on long after his assassination. (27) When Medgar Evers died in 1963, only 28,000 African Americans were registered to vote. (28) Nearly twenty years later, there were over 500,000.

1. Choose the correct way to write the underlined part of sentence 9.

   <u>Although he faced daily hardship,</u> Evers couldn't imagine leaving the southern states.

   a. Although, he faced daily hardship,
   b. Although he faced dayly hardship,
   c. Although he faces daily hardship,
   d. No change is needed.

2. Choose the sentence that could **best** be added right after sentence 14.

   a. It is not clear where Beckwith was from.
   b. Beckwith, whose fingerprints were found on the murder weapon, was tried twice.
   c. Segregation was an ongoing problem in Mississippi.
   d. Evers's brother, Charles, succeeded him as NAACP field secretary.

3. Choose the correct way to write the underlined part of sentence 1.

   Medgar Wiley Evers was born on <u>July 2 1925, near Decatur, Mississippi.</u>

   a. July 2 1925, near Decatur Mississippi.
   b. July 2, 1925, near Decatur, Mississippi.
   c. July 2 1925, near Decatur, Mississippi?
   d. No change is needed.

4. Choose the correct way to write the underlined part of sentence 19.

   Demonstrators in the black community marched after Evers's funeral procession, <u>shouting, "After Medgar, no more fear!</u>

   a. shouting, "After Medgar, no more fear!"
   b. shouting, "After Medgar, no more fear.
   c. shouts, "After Medgar, no more fear!
   d. No change is needed.

5. Which of these is **not** a complete sentence?

    a.   Evers's battle for civil rights had begun.

    b.   In a magazine article written in 1954, Evers said of the south, "I don't choose to live anywhere else.

    c.   Doing "something to be a participant and not a bystander in our society."

    d.   Nearly twenty years later, there were over 500,000.

6. Choose the correct way to write the underlined part of sentence 24.

<u>And now, Medgar, I know your gone,</u> but I'm telling you, son, it's come to pass."

    a.   And now, Medgar, I know you're gone,

    b.   And now, Medgar, I knew your gone,

    c.   And, now Medgar, I know your gone,

    d.   No change is needed.

7. Choose the correct way to write the underlined part of sentence 13.

On June 12, 1963, Evers was shot and killed <u>outside his home in Jackson Mississippi.</u>

    a.   outside his home in, Jackson Mississippi.

    b.   outside him home in Jackson Mississippi.

    c.   outside his home in Jackson, Mississippi.

    d.   No change is needed.

8. Choose the **best** way to write the underlined part of sentence 25 so that the composition maintains a consistent tone.

<u>Evers did a lot of stuff</u> for African Americans.

    a.   Mostly, Evers worked hard

    b.   Evers struggled throughout his life to end discrimination

    c.   Evers probably cared a lot about civil rights since he was an African American and that was an important issue

    d.   I guess he did stuff

9. Choose the correct way to write the underlined part of sentence 23.

    In an interview with national public radio, Charles said, "Medgar and I said many years ago, if we ever end the violent racism in this state, it'll be the greatest state in the world to live.

    a. In an interview with national public radio, Charles says,
    b. In a interview with national public radio, Charles said,
    c. In an interview with National Public Radio, Charles said,
    d. No change is needed.

10. Choose the correct way to write the underlined part of sentence 8.

    He also fought for integrated schools and organized boycotts against white-owned firms **that practiced racial discrimmanation.**

    a. that practiced, racial discrimmanation.
    b. that practiced racial discrimination.
    c. that practiced racial discrimmanation!
    d. No change is needed.

James is in the seventh grade. His teacher asked him to decide which sports team he thought was the best team ever and to write a short essay to explain why he thought the team was so great. James chose to write about the New York Yankees.

Here is James's rough draft. Read it and then answer questions 1–10.

(1) When you hear the names Babe Ruth, Lou Gehrig, Joe DiMaggio, Yogi Berra, Mickey Mantle, and Reggie Jackson what immediately comes to mind? (2) The New York Yankees, of course! (3) The New York Yankees are, in my opinion, the greatest baseball team in history and the greatest sports team ever.

(4) The New York Yankees started out as the "Highlanders" because their first stadium in New York sat on top of the highest hill in the city. (5) They were officially named the "Yankees" in 1913. (6) In 1920, they bought Babe Ruth's contract from the Boston Red Sox and started building Yankee Stadium. (7) I wish I having been there for the opening game at the stadium. (8) The Yankees beat the Red Sox 4–1, and Babe Ruth—"the Bambino"—hit his first home run in the stadium in front of 74,000 people.

(9) The Yankees have had some truly outstanding players. (10) For example, Lou Gehrig was the only player in major league history to hit twenty-three "grand slam" home runs during his career. (11) He averaged an incredible 147 runs batted in per year and, in 1931, he batted in a record 184 runs. (12) He made Most Valuable Player twice and won one Triple Crown. (13) He also contracted a disaease called Amyotrophic Lateral Sclerosis, or ALS, when he was thirty-five years old. (14) This disease was later called Lou Gehrig's Disease. (15) When Lou Gehrig got sick, the Yankees retired his number and gave him a big retirement party. (16) His number—four—was the first number ever to be retired in baseball. (17) Even though he had a fatal disease and his baseball career was over. (18) Lou Gehrig felt so grateful and proud to be one of the Yankees that he told everyone, "today I consider myself the luckiest man on the face of the earth."

(19) So far this season, the Yankees have only lost three of their last twenty-one games. (20) They have a five-and-a-half-game lead over their rival, the Boston red sox. (21) Players like Derek Jeter, Gary Sheffield, Hideki Matsui, Alex Rodriguez, Mike Mussina, Bernie Williams, and Randy Johnson are leading their team to victory. (22) There are many great ball players in the Yankees right now. (23) There are so many that the next All-Star game may have as many as five Yankees players in it. (24) That's a game I don't want to miss?

(25) Because of their great history and all the talented players who are on the team today, I think the New York Yankees are the best sports team ever. (26) If I were a professional baseball player, I would definitely want to go to work for the New York Yankees.

1. Choose the correct way to write the underlined part of sentence 4.

   <u>The New York Yankees started out as the "Highlanders"</u> because their first stadium in New York sat on top of the highest hill in the city

   a. The New York Yankees started out as the Highlanders"
   b. The New York Yankees start out as the "Highlanders"
   c. The New York yankees started out as the "Highlanders"
   d. No change is needed.

2. Which of these is **not** a complete sentence?

   a. The New York Yankees are, in my opinion, the greatest baseball team in history and the greatest sports team ever.
   b. The Yankees beat the Red Sox 4–1, and Babe Ruth—"the Bambino"—hit his first home run in the stadium in front of 74,000 people.
   c. Even though he had a fatal disease and his baseball career was over.
   d. So far this season, the Yankees have only lost three of their last twenty-one games.

3. Choose the **best** way to combine the ideas in sentences 22 and 23 into one sentence.

   There are many great ball players in the Yankees right now. There are so many that the next All-Star game may have as many as five Yankees players in it.

   a. There are so many great ball players in the Yankees right now that the next All-Star game may have as many as five Yankees players in it.
   b. Many of the great ball players in the Yankees right now will be in the All-Star game, including five players that are in it.
   c. Five Yankee players are in the All-Star game, and there may be as many great ball players in the Yankees right now.
   d. The All-Star game will definitely have five Yankee players in it, but that doesn't count all the really good players that are on the Yankees right now.

4. Choose the correct way to write the underlined part of sentence 13.

   He also <u>contracted a disaease called Amyotrophic Lateral Sclerosis,</u> or ALS, when he was thirty-five years old.

   a. contracted a disaease call Amyotrophic Lateral Sclerosis,
   b. contracted a disease called Amyotrophic Lateral Sclerosis,
   c. contracted a disaease called, Amyotrophic Lateral Sclerosis,
   d. No change is needed.

5. Choose the correct way to write the underlined part of sentence 7.

   <u>I wish I having been there</u> for the opening game at the stadium.

   a. I wish I having been their
   b. I wish I had been there
   c. Wish I having been there
   d. No change is needed.

6. Choose the correct way to write the underlined part of sentence 18.

   Lou Gehrig felt so grateful and proud to be one of the Yankees that he told everyone, <u>"today I consider myself the luckiest man on the face of the earth."</u>

   a. "Today I consider myself the luckiest man on the face of the earth."
   b. "today I consider myself the luckier man on the face of the earth."
   c. "today I consider me the luckiest man on the face of the earth."
   d. No change is needed.

7. Choose the correct way to write the underlined part of sentence 20.

   They have a five-and-a-half-game lead over <u>their rival, the Boston red sox.</u>

   a. their rival the Boston red sox.
   b. there rival, the Boston red sox.
   c. their rival, the Boston Red Sox.
   d. No change is needed.

8. Choose the word or phrase that **best** fits at the beginning of sentence 13.

    a. Luckily,
    b. For example,
    c. Unfortunately,
    d. However,

9. Choose the correct way to write the underlined part of sentence 24.

    That's a game <u>I don't want to miss?</u>

    a. I doesn't want to miss?
    b. I don't want to miss!
    c. I don't want too miss?
    d. No change is needed.

10. Choose the correct way to write the underlined part of sentence 1.

    When you hear the names Babe Ruth, Lou Gehrig, Joe DiMaggio, Yogi Berra, Mickey Mantle, and <u>Reggie Jackson what immediately comes to mind?</u>

    a. Reggie Jackson what immediately comes to mind.
    b. Reggie Jackson what immediately came to mind?
    c. Reggie Jackson, what immediately comes to mind?
    d. No change is needed.

Jutlee is in the seventh grade. Her social studies teacher asked each student to write an essay defining isolationism and imperialism, two forms of foreign policy, and then contrasting the two. Jutlee did her research, made her outline, and wrote her rough draft. Now she needs your help editing and revising it.

Here is Jutlee's rough draft. Read it and then answer questions 1–10.

(1) Imagine that you and your friend see two students having an argument on the playground. (2) You don't want to get involved because you think that the two students should work it out by themselves. (3) "Come on, let's walk away and mind our own business," you tell your friend. (4) We'll just make matters worse."

(5) "No! (6) We have to step in before somebody gets hurt. (7) I know how to handle this, and they need my advice" answers your friend. (8) Did you know that you and your friend are practicing "isolationism" and "imperialism"?

(9) Isolationism is a policy that affects the way a country relates to other countries. (10) Isolationist countries don't believe in getting too involved with other countrie's business or politics. (11) They do not like to form alliances with other countries. (12) They try very hard to be self-sufficient, and they don't want other countries to depend upon they. (13) An isolationist country believes that if it just takes care of itself, they're will be peace and prosperity. (14) At the beginning of the twentieth century before World War I, many people from the United States favored isolationism.

(15) Imperialism is a policy that is the opposite of isolationism. (16) Imperialist countries get involved in the business and politics of other countries. (17) They form economic partnerships and they depend on the relationships they have with other countries. (18) If they don't like what a country's government is doing, they try to influence that government. (19) Several imperialist countries might work together for a common goal. (20) The United States and it's allies worked together to win World War II.

(21) The United States practiced imperialism during the Vietnam War. (22) President Eisenhower warned the world against "the domino effect." (23) He was afraid that country after country was going to fall like dominoes to soviet imperialism. (24) During the Kennedy administration, the United States tried to take the control of Vietnam away from the Soviets. (25) The war continued into the Johnson administration. (26) The Vietnam War was a long, losing battle. (27) It made many Americans wish to adopt a more isolationist policy.

(28) Since the collapse of the Soviet Union, the United States has been the world's major superpower. (29) It wants to remain in power fight terrorism promote peace and do business all around the world. (30) It looked like imperialism is here to stay.

1. Choose the correct way to write the underlined part of sentence 20.

   The United States and <u>it's allies worked together to win</u> World War II.

   a. it's allies worked together too win
   b. its allies worked together to win
   c. it's allies worked together to winned
   d. No change is needed.

2. Read sentence 29, which is poorly written.

   It wants to remain in power fight terrorism promote peace and do business all around the world.

   Choose the **best** way to rewrite this sentence.

   a. It wants to remains in power fight terrorism promote peace, and do business all around the world.
   b. It wants to remain in power, fight terrorism promote peace and do business all around the World.
   c. It wants to remain in power, fight terrorism, promote peace, and do business all around the world.
   d. It wants to promote fighting and power, terrorize business, and do it all over the world.

3. Choose the correct way to write the underlined part of sentence 4.

   <u>We'll just make</u> matters worse."

   a. We'll just made
   b. "We'll just make
   c. Well just make
   d. No change is needed.

4. Choose the correct way to write the underlined part of sentence 23.

    He was afraid that country after country was <u>going to fall like dominoes to soviet imperialism.</u>

    a. going to fall like dominoes to Soviet imperialism.
    b. going to fall like dominoes to soviet Imperialism.
    c. went to fall like dominoes to soviet imperialism.
    d. No change is needed.

5. Choose the word or phrase that **best** fits at the beginning of sentence 20.

    a. However,
    b. Nevertheless,
    c. Amazingly,
    d. For example,

6. Choose the correct way to write the underlined part of sentence 7.

    I know how to handle this, and they need <u>my advice" answers your friend.</u>

    a. my advice" answers your friend?
    b. my advice" Answers your friend.
    c. my advice," answers your friend.
    d. No change is needed.

7. Choose the correct way to write the underlined part of sentence 13.

    An isolationist country believes that if it just takes care of itself, <u>they're will be peace and prosperity.</u>

    a. there will be peace and prosperity.
    b. they're will have been peace and prosperity.
    c. they're will be piece and prosperity.
    d. No change is needed.

8. Choose the correct way to write the underlined part of sentence 30.

   It looked like imperialism is here to stay.

   a. It looked like imperialism are
   b. It looks like imperialism is
   c. It looked like imperialism, is
   d. No change is needed.

9. Choose the correct way to write the underlined part of sentence 10.

   Isolationist countries don't believe in getting too involved with other countrie's business or politics.

   a. to involved with other countrie's
   b. too involved, with other countrie's
   c. too involved with other countries'
   d. No change is needed.

10. Choose the correct way to write the underlined part of sentence 12.

    They try very hard to be self-sufficient, and they don't want other countries to depend upon they.

    a. other countries to depend upon them.
    b. other countries, to depend upon they.
    c. other countries to depends upon they.
    d. No change is needed.

Kara's seventh-grade health class is studying allergies. Kara wanted to understand how an allergy works and why some people are allergic while others aren't. She went to the library and read about allergies. Then she took notes, organized them, and wrote a rough draft of a report about what causes allergies. She would like your help editing and revising it.

Here is Kara's rough draft. Read it and then answer questions 1–10.

(1) Have you ever wondered why you seem to get poison ivy every single summer, even if you stay out of the woods and don't go anywhere near a poison ivy plant? (2) Do you have a friend who can go hiking in the woods every day and has never even heard of calamine lotion? (3) When you are outside in the spring are you the one sneezing and rubbing your itchy, watery eyes while your friend looks at you with pity?

(4) Maybe you are like the lucky friend I just mentioned. (5) Then again, maybe your like me. (6) I am an allergy sufferer, and now I understand more about why me am allergic.

(7) Scientists believe that we inherit the tendency to become allergic. (8) This makes sense since my mother and father both suffer from allergies, to. (9) Scientists say that a child has a greater chance of being allergic even if only one parent has allergies. (10) Allergies are triggered when the body is exposed to an "allergen." (11) An allergen could be a food, pollen, grass, chemical, dust, dog hair, or one of many other things. (12) In people who have inherited allergies, allergens trigger nasty symptoms.

(13) Scientists believe that even people whose parents are not allergic can sometimes become allergic even if their parents are not allergic. (14) A person could become allergic if he or she is exposed to an allergen many times or for a prolonged period of time.

(15) This is how an allergy works in the body. (16) The immune system is supposed to fight bad things that attack the body. (17) When the body meets an invader, it makes special proteins called "antibodies" that fight the enemy. (18) The antibodies attach themselves to tissues and to blood cells in the body, and they wait. (19) When the invader comes along, it fits into the antibody like a key fits into a lock. (20) This tells the body's cells to make chemicals that cause redness, swelling, itching, a runny nose, and other symptoms.

(21) An allergic reaction is sort of like a false alarm. (22) The immune system gets messed up and something like dog hair causes totally huge problems. (23) That is why allergic people get the symptoms of a cold when they are exposed to an allergen. (24) Don't you wish we could tell our overeager immune systems to just relax and enjoy the great outdoors!

1.   Read sentence 13, which is poorly written.

     Scientists believe that even people whose parents are not allergic can sometimes become allergic even if their parents are not allergic.

     Choose the **best** way to rewrite this sentence.

     a.   Scientists believe that people whose parents are not allergic can become allergic no matter if their parents are allergic or not.
     b.   Scientists believe that people whose parents are not allergic can sometimes become allergic themselves.
     c.   Scientists believe that people can sometimes become allergic if their parents become allergic.
     d.   Scientists believe that people become allergic, even if their parents have not become allergic, but even if they had.

2.   Choose the correct way to write the underlined part of sentence 24.

     Don't you wish we could tell our overeager immune systems <u>to just relax and enjoy the great outdoors!</u>

     a.   to just relax and enjoy the great outdoors?
     b.   to just relax and enjoy the great, outdoors!
     c.   to just relaxes and enjoy the great outdoors!
     d.   No change is needed.

3.   Choose the correct way to write the underlined part of sentence 5.

     Then again, <u>maybe your like me.</u>

     a.   maybe your like me?
     b.   maybe your like I.
     c.   maybe you're like me.
     d.   No change is needed.

4. Kara wants to change sentence 16 so that it is more specific.

    The immune system is supposed to fight <u>bad things that attack</u> the body.

    Choose the **best** way to rewrite the underlined part of this sentence.

    a. bad things and other junk that attack
    b. harmful things like viruses and bacteria that attack
    c. stuff that attacks
    d. back against things attacking

5. Choose the correct way to write the underlined part of sentence 3.

    <u>When you are outside in the spring are you</u> the one sneezing and rubbing your itchy, watery eyes while your friend looks at you with pity?

    a. When, you are outside in the spring are you
    b. When you are outside in the spring, are you
    c. When your outside in the spring are you
    d. No change is needed.

6. Choose the correct way to write the underlined part of sentence 8.

    This makes sense since my <u>mother and father both suffer from allergies, to.</u>

    a. Mother and Father both suffer from allergies, to.
    b. mother and father both suffer, from allergies, to.
    c. mother and father both suffer from allergies, too.
    d. No change is needed.

7. Choose the sentence that could **best** be added right after sentence 14.

    a. A person could become allergic if he or she is exposed to an allergen over an extended period.
    b. Allergies are a hassle.
    c. Scientists have been studying allergens.
    d. A florist who works in a flower shop every day might become allergic to roses, for example.

8. Choose the correct way to write the underlined part of sentence 6.

I am an allergy sufferer, and now <u>I understand more about why me am allergic.</u>

    a.   I understand more about why I am allergic.
    b.   I understood more about why me am allergic.
    c.   I understand more about why me are allergic.
    d.   No change is needed.

9. Kara wants to add this sentence to the paragraph that begins with sentence 7.

An allergen is anything that causes an allergic reaction in the body.

Where would the sentence **best** fit?

    a.   right after sentence 7
    b.   right after sentence 9
    c.   right after sentence 10
    d.   right after sentence 12

10. Choose the **best** way to write the underlined part of sentence 22 so that the composition maintains a consistent tone.

The immune system <u>gets messed up and something like dog hair causes totally huge problems.</u>

    a.   gets messes up and dog hair is a big issue.
    b.   encounters big problems from dog hairs and other junk.
    c.   can't handle all the crazy allergens in the air, even something like dog hair.
    d.   malfunctions and treats a harmless allergen, such as dog hair, like an enemy invader.

Lynn's seventh-grade history class is studying Alexander the Great. Her teacher asks each student to choose a topic somehow relating to Alexander the Great and his conquests and to write a report on it. Lynn has written her outline and rough draft. She needs your help editing and revising it.

Here is Lynn's rough draft. Read it and then answer questions 1–10.

---

(1) Thousands of years ago, astrology was only for members of royalty. (2) An astrologer could look forward to a comfortable life if he or she was well liked. (3) If the court astrologer's news made the royal benefactor angry, the astrologer would most likely lose his or her head.

(4) Western Tropical astronomy dates from ancient Mesopotamia around 2300 B.C.E. (5) It made it's way to ancient Greece in about 600 B.C.E. (6) In fact, the first astrologers appeared in Greece with the first philosophers, men such as Socrates, Plato, and Aristotle. (7) Alexander the Great was a student of Aristotle. (8) Therefore, between 336 B.C.E. and 323 B.C.E., he spread Greek culture and thought over a much wider area as he conquered other lands.

(9) From 323 B.C.E. to 31 B.C.E., Alexandria Egypt, became the center of Greek thought and philosophy. (10) During this time, astrology did well among important thinkers of this time. (11) Horoscopes, zodiac signs, and individual astrological readings appeared. (12) Astrology was no longer just for royalty.

(13) During the Middle Ages, the popularity of astrology began to fade in the Western world. (14) It made a comeback during the European Renaissance, which lasted in some places until the 1670s. (15) Men such as Marsilio Ficino were practicing Catholics, astrologers, and philosophers. (16) Scientists figured out in the seventeenth century that Earth was not the center of the universe, astrology suffered a terrible blow. (17) Meanwhile, astronomy became more important.

(18) Less than two hundred years ago, astrology in Western society gained in popularity once again. (19) Astrologers Sepharial (1860–1917) and Alan Leo (1864–1929) were fascinating, energetic, and mysterious. (20) They drew peoples' interest and founded the Theosophical Society in Great Britain. (21) In the twentieth century, ideas like karma, reincarnation, and daily horoscopes became extremely popular. (22) Astrologer Paul Clancy's magazine, *American Astrology* became a huge success in 1934. (23) *American Astrology*'s reputation is believed to have sparked people's interest in daily and weekly astrological columns. (24) They commonly appear in newspapers and magazines in the United States today. (25) They also show up in newspapers and magazines in Great Britain.

1. Read sentence 8, which is poorly written.

   Therefore, between 336 B.C.E. and 323 B.C.E., he spread Greek culture and thought over a much wider area as he conquered other lands.

   Choose the **best** way to rewrite this sentence.

   a. Greek culture and thought were spread over other lands between 336 B.C.E. and 323 B.C.E. since Alexander the Great was Greek.
   b. Therefore, he spread Greek culture and thought over a much wider area as he conquered other lands between 336 B.C.E. and 323 B.C.E., since he was a student of Aristotle.
   c. Between 336 B.C.E. and 323 B.C.E., his conquest of other lands spread Greek culture and thought over a much wider area.
   d. By conquering other lands between 336 B.C.E. and 323 B.C.E., he spread wide Greek culture and thought.

2. Choose the word or phrase that **best** fits at the beginning of sentence 3.

   a. However,
   b. For example,
   c. Therefore,
   d. Consequently,

3. Choose the correct way to write the underlined part of sentence 20.

   <u>They drew peoples' interest</u> and founded the Theosophical Society in Great Britain.

   a. Them drew peoples' interest
   b. They drew people's interest
   c. They drawed peoples' interest
   d. No change is needed.

4. Choose the correct way to write the underlined part of sentence 6.

   In fact, the first astrologers <u>appeared in Greece with the first philosophers,</u> men such as Socrates, Plato, and Aristotle.

   a. appeared in Greece with the first Philosophers,
   b. appeared in Greece, with the first philosophers,
   c. appears in Greece with the first philosophers,
   d. No change is needed.

5. Read sentence 10, which is poorly written.

During this time, astrology did well among important thinkers of this time.

Choose the **best** way to rewrite this sentence.

   a. During this time, astrology did good among important thinkers of this time.
   b. During this time, astrology did well among important thinkers.
   c. During this time, important thinkers did well with astrology.
   d. During this time, astrology was good and well among important thinkers of this time.

6. Choose the correct way to write the underlined part of sentence 5.

It made it's way to ancient Greece in about 600 B.C.E.

   a. It made its way to ancient Greece
   b. It made it's way to Ancient Greece
   c. It made it's way too ancient Greece
   d. No change is needed.

7. Read sentence 16, which is poorly written.

Scientists figured out in the seventeenth century that Earth was not the center of the universe, astrology suffered a terrible blow.

Choose the **best** way to rewrite this sentence.

   a. Scientists, in the seventeenth century, knew that Earth was not the center of the Universe, so astrology suffered a terrible blow.
   b. In the seventeenth century, scientists figured out that Earth was not the center of the universe, astrology suffered a terrible blow.
   c. Astrology suffered a terrible blow when scientists figured out that earth was not the center of the Universe in the seventeenth century.
   d. When scientists figured out in the seventeenth century that Earth was not the center of the universe, astrology suffered a terrible blow.

8. Choose the correct way to write the underlined part of sentence 9.

    From 323 B.C.E. <u>to 31 B.C.E., Alexandria Egypt, became</u> the center of Greek thought and philosophy.

    a. to 31 B.C.E., Alexandria Egypt, become
    b. to 31 B.C.E. Alexandria Egypt, became
    c. to 31 B.C.E., Alexandria, Egypt, became
    d. No change is needed.

9. Choose the **best** way to combine the ideas in sentences 24 and 25 into one sentence.

    They commonly appear in newspapers and magazines in the United States today. They also show up in newspapers and magazines in Great Britain.

    a. Great Britain's newspapers and magazines commonly have them and so do the United States'.
    b. The United States and Great Britain both appear in newspapers and magazines today.
    c. The United States' newspapers and magazines commonly feature them as well as do Great Britain's newspapers and magazines.
    d. Today, they commonly appear in newspapers and magazines in both the United States and Great Britain.

10. Choose the correct way to write the underlined part of sentence 22.

    <u>Astrologer Paul Clancy's magazine, *American Astrology* became</u> a huge success in 1934.

    a. Astrologer Paul Clancys' magazine, *American Astrology* became
    b. Astrologer Paul Clancy's magazine, *American Astrology*, became
    c. Astrologer Paul Clancy's Magazine, *American Astrology* became
    d. No change is needed.

Hector's seventh-grade social studies class is doing a unit on health and the emotions. He has been asked to write an imaginary letter to a friend who has been showing an emotional behavior and describe how this behavior is affecting the friend's life. Hector chooses to write about anger. He does some research, writes an outline, and constructs his rough draft. He needs your help editing and revising it.

Here is Hector's rough draft. Read it and then answer questions 1–10.

(1) Dear Chloe

(2) I am writing this letter to you because I have noticed that you have been acting particularly angry over the past few weeks. (3) I think I can help you to better understand the source of your anger and how to manage it.

(4) Anger is a normal, healthy human emotion. (5) Unless it gets out of control. (6) It can lead to problems at home, at school, and with your friends. (7) It can also make you feel like you don't have control over your life. (8) Sometimes, I think you feel this way. (9) Anger causes a person's heart rate and blood pressure rates to go up. (10) His or her adrenaline and hormone levels increase as well.

(11) You may not even be clear as to why your so upset all the time. (12) It could be that you're angry with a specific person, like a friend, family member, or teacher. (13) You could be mad about an event, such as failing a test or missing the bus. (14) Also, memories of trauma can cause anger.

(15) Many times, people use aggression to express their anger. (16) However, you can't lash out at every person or thing, that makes you mad or annoys you. (17) Laws, society, and common sense will tell you that. (18) There are a few ways that you can manage your anger to kept a better handle on it in the future.

(19) Expressing your angry feelings in a non-aggressive, assertive way is the healthiest way to relieve yourself of the emotion. (20) You must learn to communicate your needs to others in a clear, positive, respectful way. (21) Some people use a different technique: suppression. (22) The goal is to convert the anger into constructive behavior. (23) However, suppression often leads to tense, depressed feelings, and high blood pressure. (24) Another way to control your anger is to calm down inside. (25) By controlling your external and internal responses and taking steps to lower your heart rate, the feelings will generally decrease.

(26) Unexpressed anger can cause many problems. (27) People who constantly put others down, criticize everything, and make cynical comments haven't learned how to express their anger constructively. (28) Unfortunately, they seldom have positive relationships with others. (29) You can be a real jerk sometimes, so I wanted to tell you this.

(continued on next page)

(continued from previous page)

(30) The best step you can take is to identify what makes you angry and than develop strategies to keep you from going over the edge. (31) Life is filled with frustration, loss, pain, and unpredictability. (32) By changing the way events and people affect you—thereby minimizing angry and frustrated reactions—you'll enjoy a much happier life.

(33) sincerely yours,

(34) Hector

1. Choose the correct way to write line 33, the closing of the letter.

   sincerely yours,

   a. sincerely yours.
   b. Sincerely yours,
   c. sinseerly yours,
   d. No change is needed.

2. Hector wants to add this sentence to the paragraph that begins with sentence 19.

   If you hold in your anger, stop thinking about it, and focus on something positive, you are using suppression.

   Where would the sentence **best** fit?

   a. right after sentence 20
   b. right after sentence 21
   c. right after sentence 23
   d. right after sentence 24

3. Choose the correct way to write the underlined part of sentence 11.

   You may not even <u>be clear as to why your so upset</u> all the time.

   a. be clear as to why you're so upset
   b. be clear as to why your so upsetted
   c. be clear, as to why your so upset
   d. No change is needed.

4. Which of these is **not** a complete sentence?

   a. Unless it gets out of control.
   b. Laws, society, and common sense will tell you that.
   c. Unfortunately, they seldom have positive relationships with others.
   d. By changing the way events and people affect you—thereby minimizing angry and frustrated reactions—you'll enjoy a much happier life.

5. Choose the correct way to write the underlined part of sentence 16.

   However, you can't lash out at every <u>person or thing, that makes you mad</u> or annoys you.

   a. person or thing, that makes you mad,
   b. person or thing, that made you mad
   c. person or thing that makes you mad
   d. No change is needed.

6. Choose the correct way to write line 1, the opening of the letter.

   Dear Chloe

   a. Dear Chloe.
   b. Dear Chloe,
   c. Deer Chloe
   d. No change is needed.

7. Choose the **best** way to write the underlined part of sentence 29 so that the composition maintains a consistent tone.

   <u>You can be a real jerk sometimes,</u> so I wanted to tell you this.

   a. It's not like I care, but it would be really annoying if you got like that,
   b. Listen up, you have a tendency to be really irritating and bad-tempered,
   c. You waste time being mean to everybody,
   d. I don't want to see that happen to you,

8. Choose the correct way to write the underlined part of sentence 30.

    The best step you can take is to identify what makes you angry and <u>than develop strategies to keep you</u> from going over the edge.

    a. then develop strategies to keep you
    b. than develop strageties to keep you
    c. than develop strategies to kept you
    d. No change is needed.

9. Choose the correct way to write the underlined part of sentence 18.

    There are a few ways that you can <u>manage your anger to kept a better handle</u> on it in the future.

    a. manages your anger to kept a better handle
    b. manage you're anger to kept a better handle
    c. manage your anger to keep a better handle
    d. No change is needed.

10. Choose the sentence that could **best** be added right after sentence 30.

    a. If you're feeling sad and lonely, just get angry and you'll feel better.
    b. If you need to talk to someone about it, go to an adult who seems really mad all the time, so they can understand that there are other people out there like them.
    c. Follow a set plan to find your way to happiness, such as getting really mad and breaking stuff that belongs to your friends.
    d. Change the way you think, use silliness and laughter to brighten a tense moment, or give yourself a break from the situation or environment that is triggering your anger.

118

Eric's seventh-grade social studies teacher has requested that each student write a report expressing his or her opinion on the following question: *If you were having difficulty with a certain subject in school, do you think you would learn better from one of your peers or from an adult instructor?* Eric made a web of ideas for and against peer tutoring and wrote his report. He needs your help editing and revising it.

Here is Eric's rough draft. Read it and then answer questions 1–10.

---

(1) If I was having trouble in a certain subject, I think it would be usefuller to get help from someone my age. (2) In researching this topic, I learned that students gain many helpful skills through peer tutoring. (3) Tutoring benefits both the tutor and the other student (the tutee).

(4) I've learned that students become stronger in academics. (5) Meanwhile, there social behaviors, classroom discipline, and relationships improve as well. (6) Plus, peer tutoring could led more students to want to enter teaching later on in life. (7) The skills learned in peer tutoring could also turn into good parenting skills.

(8) Peer tutoring in math and language arts bennefits both the tutor and the tutee. (9) Mostly, the tutors gain further skills in understanding the subject matter. (10) Tutees earn higher grades in the subjects, while better understanding the subject as a whole. (11) I'm pretty good at math.

(12) One reason peer tutoring is so effective is because kids all speak the same language. (13) The tutee feels like he or she is on the same level as the tutor. (14) The tutee is more likely to do certain things in front of another student. (15) Communication between the two students is probably more casual and more balanced. (16) Therefore, the fact that the tutor is in a position of higher status doesn't mean as much in peer tutoring.

(17) Those students working as tutors have to be trained in how to do it correctly. (18) No matter what their academic skills, they must understand that they have a responsibility to the students working under they as tutees. (19) Teachers must be involved in this process. (20) Therefore, peer tutoring still involves adult supervision. (21) Tutors will form a better relationship with the student they're tutoring, who learn to be responsible, capable models for their tutees.

(22) Tutees gain a firmer understanding of the subject they am struggling with. (23) Tutoring teaches about fairness and improves self-esteem. (24) It makes kids more willing to share and be kind to others. (25) Peer tutoring boosts communication and develops creative and critical-thinking skills.

(26) Through the research I've done, I've learned that peer tutoring could be good. (27) I feel that it would be more rewarding and fun to be tutored by someone with whom I have more in common.

1. Eric wants to change sentence 14 so that it is more specific.

   The tutee is more likely to <u>do certain things</u> in front of another student.

   Choose the **best** way to rewrite the underlined part of this sentence.

   a. speak freely
   b. feel at ease
   c. relax
   d. ask questions, give opinions, and risk guessing the wrong answer

2. Choose the correct way to write the underlined part of sentence 1.

   If I was having trouble in a certain subject, <u>I think it would be usefuller to get help</u> from someone my age.

   a. I think it would be more useful to get help
   b. I thought it would be usefuller to get help
   c. I think it would been usefuller to get help
   d. No change is needed.

3. Choose the correct way to write the underlined part of sentence 6.

   Plus, <u>peer tutoring could led more students</u> to want to enter teaching later on in life.

   a. peer tutoring could led more student's
   b. peer tutoring, could led more students
   c. peer tutoring could lead more students
   d. No change is needed.

4. Choose the sentence that does **not** belong in the paragraph that begins with sentence 8.

   a. sentence 8
   b. sentence 9
   c. sentence 10
   d. sentence 11

5. Choose the correct way to write the underlined part of sentence 5.

   Meanwhile, there social behaviors, classroom discipline, and relationships improve as well.

   a. Mean while, there social behaviors,
   b. Meanwhile, their social behaviors,
   c. Meanwhile, there social behavyors,
   d. No change is needed.

6. Choose the correct way to write the underlined part of sentence 18.

   No matter what their academic skills, they must understand that they have a responsibility to the students working under they as tutees.

   a. students' working under they as tutees.
   b. students working under them as tutees.
   c. students working under they as tutees?
   d. No change is needed.

7. Read sentence 21, which is poorly written.

   Tutors will form a better relationship with the student they're tutoring, who learn to be responsible, capable models for their tutees.

   Choose the **best** way to rewrite this sentence.

   a. Tutors who learn to be responsible, capable models for their tutees will form a better relationship with them.
   b. Tutors will form a better relationship with their tutees if they form a better relationship.
   c. Tutors and tutees will have a better relationship if they learn to be responsible, capable models for each other.
   d. Tutors will learn to be responsible, capable models while they are forming a better relationship with their tutees.

121

8. Choose the correct way to write the underlined part of sentence 8.

Peer <u>tutoring in math and language arts bennefits</u> both the tutor and the tutee.

    a. tutoring in math and language arts' bennefits
    b. tutoring in math and language arts benefits
    c. tutor in math and language arts bennefits
    d. No change is needed.

9. Choose the correct way to write the underlined part of sentence 22.

Tutees gain a firmer understanding <u>of the subject they am struggling with.</u>

    a. of the subject them am struggling with.
    b. of the subject, they am struggling with.
    c. of the subject they are struggling with.
    d. No change is needed.

10. Read sentence 26, which is poorly written.

Through the research I've done, I've learned that peer tutoring could be good.

Choose the **best** way to rewrite this sentence.

    a. Peer tutoring is good, and I know that because I've done a lot of research.
    b. Through the research I've done, I learned that peer tutoring can work out pretty well.
    c. I've done a lot of research and have come to the conclusion that peer tutoring could be good because I've done research on that.
    d. Through the research I've done, I've learned the many benefits of peer tutoring.

Josephine's school had a Career Day for the seventh grade. Following this special event, each student was asked to submit a short report describing the career he or she had found most interesting. Josephine liked the presentation about becoming a film critic the most, so she outlined her ideas and wrote a rough draft on that subject. She needs your help editing and revising it.

Here is Josephine's rough draft. Read it and then answer questions 1–10.

(1) I found the film criticism segment of today's Career Day to be the most fascinating. (2) The best thing about being a film critic is that anyone who loves movies can enjoy doing it. (3) Ellen Simmons seemed to get a lot out of her work, who gave the talk on being a film critic. (4) She said that she never dreaded sitting down to watch a movie, so why shouldn't she enjoy being a film critic! (5) I have to say that it sounds pretty good to me.

(6) Mrs. Simmons recommends that a student wanting to work as a film critic for a newspaper should become a journalist first. (7) In the meantime, the person should continuously write about film whenever he or she can. (8) She also thinks that watching movies on the "big screen" gave her a much better perspective on the films she were seeing. (9) Watching movies at home didn't seem to be quite as effective at giving her an impression of the movie.

(10) Once you become a film critic, Mrs. Simmons says that the best way to critique a film is by staying objective. (11) She doesn't pay attention to the stars cast in the movie or the director or the stars that are in it. (12) She rarely listens to other people's opinions on the film. (13) She focuses her complete attention on the movie itself.

(14) Some students asked Mrs. Simmons, if she thought writing in the first person (using "I") in film criticisms was a wise idea. (15) Mrs. Simmons felt that writing in the first person was perfectly acceptable and maybe even more enjoyable reading. (16) Since the writer could display a bit more personality as he or she wrote. (17) She warned, however, that writing criticisms in first person left the writer open to personal attacks from displeased readers. (18) He or she could expect very favorable responses from readers who agreed with the criticism.

(19) A common trick used to show that you are knowledgeable about movies of all kinds and from all times is to compare films from the past to the movie you are currently critiquing. (20) Mrs. Simmons recommends including these comparisons frequently in writing. (21) However, if you do not possess this kind of knowledge of movie history, don't fake it. (22) You're wiser readers will know.

(23) Film critics write to many audiences. (24) Their work is often in college newspapers, daily, weekly, or monthly publications, and on websites. (25) No matter who is in your audience, you want to write clearly. (26) You never know who may be reading your piece.

(27) Mrs. Simmons not only got me exited about being a film critic. (28) She also made me want to write a film criticism column for our school newspaper!

1. Choose the correct way to write the underlined part of sentence 27.

   Mrs. Simmons not only <u>got me exited about being a film critic.</u>

   a. got I exited about being a film critic.
   b. got me exited about being a film critic?
   c. got me excited about being a film critic.
   d. No change is needed.

2. Read sentence 3, which is poorly written.

   Ellen Simmons seemed to get a lot out of her work, who gave the talk on being a film critic.

   Choose the **best** way to rewrite this sentence.

   a. Ellen Simmons, who gave the talk on being a film critic, seemed to get a lot out of her work.
   b. Ellen Simmons seemed to get a lot out of the talk on being a film critic.
   c. Ellen Simmons's film critic gave a talk and seemed to get a lot out of her work.
   d. Ellen Simmons's work as a film critic gave a talk on being a film critic and her work.

3. Read sentence 11, which is poorly written.

   She doesn't pay attention to the stars cast in the movie or the director or the stars that are in it.

   Choose the **best** way to rewrite it so that it does not repeat ideas.

   a. She doesn't pay attention to neither the stars cast in the movie nor the director.
   b. She doesn't pay attention to the director, the stars cast in the movie, or the stars in the movie.
   c. She doesn't pay attention to the stars cast in the movie, the movie, or the director.
   d. She doesn't pay attention to the stars cast in the movie or to the director.

4. Choose the correct way to write the underlined part of sentence 8.

   She also thinks that watching movies on the "big screen" gave her a much better <u>perspective on the films she were seeing.</u>

   a. perspecktive on the films she were seeing.
   b. perspective on the films she was seeing.
   c. perspective on the films she were "seeing."
   d. No change is needed.

5. Choose the correct way to write the underlined part of sentence 4.

   She said that she never dreaded sitting down to watch a movie, so <u>why shouldn't she enjoy being a film critic!</u>

   a. why shouldn't she enjoy being a film critic?
   b. why shouldn't, she enjoy being a film critic!
   c. why shouldn't she enjoy to be a film critic!
   d. No change is needed.

6. Which of these is **not** a complete sentence?

   a. I have to say that it sounds pretty good to me.
   b. Since the writer could display a bit more personality as he or she wrote.
   c. You're wiser readers will know.
   d. No matter who is in your audience, you want to write clearly.

7. Choose the correct way to write the underlined part of sentence 14.

   Some students <u>asked Mrs. Simmons, if she thought writing</u> in the first person (using "I") in film criticisms was a wise idea.

   a. asked Mrs. Simmons, if she thought wrote
   b. asked Mrs. Simmons if she thought writing
   c. asked mrs. Simmons, if she thought writing
   d. No change is needed.

8. Read sentence 9, which is poorly written.

Watching movies at home didn't seem to be quite as effective at giving her an impression of the movie.

Choose the **best** way to rewrite this sentence.

   a. Watching movies at home, as effective as it was at giving her an impression of the movie, didn't seem to be as effective.
   b. Watching movies at home did not leave her with as effectively impressed upon the movie.
   c. Watching movies at home, on the other hand, didn't seem to be quite as effective.
   d. Effectively impressed with movies as she was, watching them at home just didn't do it quite as well.

9. Choose the correct way to write the underlined part of sentence 22.

   <u>You're wiser readers</u> will know.

   a. You're wizer readers
   b. Your wiser readers
   c. You're wiser readers'
   d. No change is needed.

10. Choose the word or phrase that **best** fits at the beginning of sentence 18.

   a. On the other hand,
   b. Fortunately,
   c. For instance,
   d. Amazingly,

Christian's social studies class has been studying social pressures. His teacher has asked that each student write a persuasive report on something in contemporary society that influences teenagers. Christian visits his library, writes an outline, and writes his report. He needs your help editing and revising it.

Here is Christian's rough draft. Read it and then answer questions 1–10.

(1) Advertising is a powerful form of communication. (2) Without even realizing it, an average American sees over 5,000 advertisements every day. (3) Advertisers in the United States must keep up with the trends and interests of the entire population. (4) What they have learned over time, however, is the incredible buying power of the teenage consumer. (5) Is advertising just a means of selling a product, or is it a way to manipulate people as well.

(6) Advertisers do their research. (7) They watch what we do, what we're interested in, and what we hope one day to be. (8) By conducting surveys on the phone and written questionnaires and offering samples of their products advertisers get an idea of how the average American reacts to what is being sold. (9) These kinds of research is necessary in advertising. (10) However, not all the methods advertisers employ are moral.

(11) Advertisers commonly use people's fears and insecurities to get them to buy products. (12) Pharmaceutical company's television ads, for example, could lead people to believe that they need the advertised drugs. (13) In fact, those people could be in perfect health.

(14) Teenagers are the top consumers in today's society, so many advertisers have shifted their focus to target them. (15) Many teenagers have part-time jobs and do not have bills to pay. (16) Therefore, their money is mainly spent on leisure activities, such as shopping and going to the movies. (17) Advertisers may also enjoy these activities.

(18) Since teenagers are constantly changing the advertising industry tries to change with them. (19) Most teenagers want to be individuals. (20) At the same time, they don't want to be too separate from the group. (21) They usually have this "life is good" attitude and then spend their money without using their brains. (22) Keeping up with changing trends is also important to many teenagers, which leads advertisers to pitch to them even more aggressively. (23) Advertisers will make original, flashy, and funny ads to appeal to teenagers. (24) They will use popular music and dancing. (25) Not too long ago, the Gap became the most fashionable clothing store because of the popularity of their swing music commercials.

(26) Celebrities often appeal to teenagers. (27) Therefore, advertisers create ads and brands endorsed by celebrities. (28) People are often mistakenly led to believe that certain products will bringing about popularity and happiness. (29) Nike ads, for example, often portray star athletes wearing the nike brand. (30) Is it the shoes that made the athlete popular? (31) Certainly not.

(continued on next page)

(continued from previous page)

(32) The advertising industry can be harmful to teenagers. (33) It teaches impulsive spending habits. (34) It also teaches that popularity and fitting in are more important than individuality. (35) Advertising may be misleading and in some cases immoral. (36) Nevertheless, consumers must learn to make intelligent buying decisions.

1. Choose the correct way to write the underlined part of sentence 29.

    Nike ads, for example, often portray <u>star athletes wearing the nike brand.</u>

    a. star athleets wearing the nike brand.
    b. star athletes wearing the Nike brand.
    c. star athletes wears the nike brand.
    d. No change is needed.

2. Choose the sentence that does **not** belong in the paragraph that begins with sentence 14.

    a. sentence 14
    b. sentence 15
    c. sentence 16
    d. sentence 17

3. Choose the **best** way to write the underlined part of sentence 21 so that the composition maintains a consistent tone.

    <u>They usually have this "life is good" attitude and then</u> spend their money without using their brains.

    a. They wonder why everything is so great all the time when they
    b. They're like, "Hey, everything's cool," and then
    c. They are often optimistic and like to impulsively
    d. They have a good attitude, which leads them to think it is a bad idea to

4. Choose the correct way to write the underlined part of sentence 5.

    Is advertising just a means of selling a product, or is it <u>a way to manipulate people as well.</u>

    a. a way to manipulate people as well?
    b. a way to manipulate people's as well.
    c. a way to manipulate people as good.
    d. No change is needed.

128

5. Choose the correct way to write the underlined part of sentence 12.

   <u>Pharmaceutical company's television ads,</u> for example, could lead people to believe that they need the advertised drugs.

   a. Pharmaceutical company's television adds,
   b. Pharmaceutical companies' television ads,
   c. Pharmaceutical Company's television ads,
   d. No change is needed.

6. Choose the correct way to write the underlined part of sentence 28.

   People are often mistakenly <u>led to believe that certain products will bringing</u> about popularity and happiness.

   a. led to believe that certain products will bring
   b. lead to believe that certain products will bringing
   c. led to believe that certain product's will bringing
   d. No change is needed.

7. Read sentence 8, which is poorly written.

   By conducting surveys on the phone and written questionnaires and offering samples of their products advertisers get an idea of how the average American reacts to what is being sold.

   Choose the **best** way to rewrite this sentence.

   a. Conducting surveys over the phone and written questionnaires over the phone and offering samples over the phone will let advertisers get an idea of how the average American reacts to what is being sold.
   b. With phones, questionnaires, and samples, advertisers will get an idea of how the average American reacts to what is being sold.
   c. Conducting surveys on the phone and written questionnaires, offering samples of their products, advertisers get an idea of how the average American reacts to what is being sold.
   d. By conducting phone surveys, taking written questionnaires, and offering samples of their products, advertisers get an idea of how the average American reacts to what is being sold.

8. Choose the correct way to write the underlined part of sentence 18.

    <u>Since teenagers are constantly changing</u> the advertising industry tries to change with them.

    a. Since teenagers' are constantly changing
    b. Since teenagers are constantly changes
    c. Since teenagers are constantly changing,
    d. No change is needed.

9. Choose the correct way to write the underlined part of sentence 9.

    <u>These kinds of research is</u> necessary in advertising.

    a. These kinds of researchs is
    b. These kinds of research are
    c. These kinds' of research is
    d. No change is needed.

10. Read sentence 22, which is poorly written.

    Keeping up with changing trends is also important to many teenagers, which leads advertisers to pitch to them even more aggressively.

    Choose the **best** way to rewrite this sentence.

    a. Because many teenagers try to keep up with changing trends, advertisers will pitch to them even more aggressively.
    b. Thinking that keeping up with trends is important, teenagers and advertisers pitch to them even more aggressively.
    c. Keeping up with changing trends is also important to teenagers so that advertisers will pitch to them even more aggressively.
    d. Aggressively pitching to teenagers to keep up with changing trends will make teenagers pitch them.

Kynara's seventh-grade history class is writing reports about topics relating to twentieth-century United States' history. Kynara chooses to write about the history of snowboarding. She composes an outline and writes her rough draft. She needs your help editing and revising it.

Here is Kynara's rough draft. Read it and then answer questions 1–10.

(1) Skiing has been around in the United States since the early twentieth century. (2) Since that time, the retail industry dealing in Winter sports has steadily grown. (3) In the 1990s, it skyrocketed. (4) For the first time in history, snowboarding was the cause.

(5) Snowboarding first appeared in 1972. (6) A fifteen-year-old kid named Jake Burton decided that he was bored with skiing and wanted to try something new. (7) He built his first snowboard in about three weeks. (8) Burton take his new invention to the nearby ski slopes to test it out. (9) Unfortunately, he was denied access time and time again. (10) Burton didn't need a professional ski slope to practice on his prototype snowboard, however. (11) He continued to try to gain access to ski slopes, but had no luck. (12) He realized that the only way to prove what his invention could do was to make a video of himself riding it.

(13) Burton met Craig Kelly shortly thereafter. (14) When he heard about Burton's idea, Kelly enthusiastically offered to produce his video. (15) In the meantime, Burton had built several more snowboards that his closest friends had been riding. (16) Burton and Kelly took they're video to the ski slopes and showed it around. (17) They finally met with success at Okemo, whose management agreed to allow Burton to ride during the week. (18) Burton snowboards, inc., was born.

(19) In the 1980s, the growth of snowboarding was slow and many ski slopes still would not allow snowboarders on their trails. (20) In the 1990s, Generation X made many things popular. (21) Snowboarding rapidly became the next big thing in winter sports. (22) By 1991, as many as 85 percent of all ski resorts allowed snowboarders to share the slopes with skiers.

(23) Soon, problems arose between skiers and snowboarders. (24) There were more accidents as snowboarders practicing their tricks on the slopes—and often fall down trying—got in the way of skiers simply making their way down the mountain. (25) Parks designed exclusively for snowboarders began popping up across the country.

(26) Snowboarding brought with it an new, original image. (27) Snowboarders dressed differently and had different hairstyles. (28) The theme of the 1990s was being different. (29) Snowboarding fit right in. (30) It wasn't just the resort industry that was capitalizing on the new sport. (31) Retail outlets were also greatly benefiting from the new business. (32) Snowboarding equipment was often cheaper than ski equipment, so many younger people could afford it. (33) Snowboarding lessons became another profitable business.

(34) Snowboarding seems to only be gaining in popularity. (35) It brings with it a fresh, independent spirit that almost anyone can enjoy.

1. Kynara wants to change sentence 20 so that it is more specific.

   In the 1990s, Generation X made <u>many things popular.</u>

   Choose the **best** way to rewrite the underlined part of this sentence.

   a. lots of stuff popular.
   b. skateboarding, BMX, bungee jumping, and rollerblading popular.
   c. many things they liked become popular.
   d. a ton of activities that made them happy.

2. Choose the correct way to write the underlined part of sentence 18.

   <u>Burton snowboards, inc.,</u> was born.

   a. Burton snowboards, ink,
   b. burton snowboards, inc.,
   c. Burton Snowboards, Inc.,
   d. No change is needed.

3. Choose the correct way to write the underlined part of sentence 8.

   <u>Burton take his new invention to the</u> nearby ski slopes to test it out.

   a. Burton take his knew invention to the
   b. Burton take his new invention two the
   c. Burton took his new invention to the
   d. No change is needed.

4. Choose the correct way to write the underlined part of sentence 32.

   Snowboarding equipment was often <u>cheaper than ski equipment,</u> so many younger people could afford it.

   a. cheaper then ski equipment,
   b. cheaper than ski equiptment,
   c. more cheaper than ski equipment,
   d. No change is needed.

5. Choose the correct way to write the underlined part of sentence 2.

   Since that time, the retail industry dealing in <u>Winter sports has steadily grown.</u>

   a. Winter sports has steadily growed.
   b. winter sports has steadily grown.
   c. Winter sport's has steadily grown.
   d. No change is needed.

6. Choose the sentence that could **best** be added right after sentence 13.

   a. Kelly was already filming skateboarding and skiing videos.
   b. Burton was fifteen years old in 1972.
   c. Even then, snowboarding was still fairly new.
   d. Skiing was still popular at this time.

7. Choose the correct way to write the underlined part of sentence 26.

   Snowboarding brought with it <u>an new, original image.</u>

   a. a new, original image.
   b. an new, original images.
   c. an new, original, image.
   d. No change is needed.

8. Kynara wants to add this sentence to the paragraph that begins with sentence 5.

   He trekked along backcountry trails instead to learn what the snowboard could do.

   Where would the sentence **best** fit?

   a. right after sentence 5
   b. right after sentence 7
   c. right after sentence 9
   d. right after sentence 10

9. Choose the correct way to write the underlined part of sentence 24.

    There were more accidents as snowboarders practicing their tricks on the slopes—<u>and often fall down trying</u>—got in the way of skiers simply making their way down the mountain.

    a. and often fall down tryng
    b. and often falling down trying
    c. and often, fall down trying
    d. No change is needed.

10. Choose the correct way to write the underlined part of sentence 16.

    Burton and Kelly <u>took they're video to</u> the ski slopes and showed it around.

    a. had taken they're video to
    b. took they're video too
    c. took their video to
    d. No change is needed.

134

The seventh-grade class has been learning about health. Each student has been asked to write a report about a specific health issue. Pete does some research at the local library, makes a web of ideas, and writes his rough draft. He needs your help editing and revising it.

Here is Pete's rough draft. Read it and then answer questions 1–10.

(1) Eating disorders have been a common issue in women's health. (2) Women aren't the only ones unhappy with their looks, however. (3) Some of these same disorders now affect men in the United States, such as anorexia nervosa and bulimia. (4) In fact, as many as one million men suffer from eating disorders.

(5) Many males may think that they are compulsive eaters. (6) They may actually have a binge eating disorder like bulimia. (7) "Bulimia" involves rapidly eating lots of food and than vomiting it up to prevent weight gain. (8) Sufferers of "anorexia nervosa," on the other hand, stop eating because they are afraid of gaining weight. (9) Symptoms of this disorder include nervousness combined with lose of appetite.

(10) Males with these disorders tend to be more active. (11) They are also usually anxious about food, and weight. (12) Teasing can lead a man to develop an eating disorder. (13) He may also fear weight-related illnesses found in other family members or want to remove extra flab from part of his body. (14) Both men and women with eating disorders want to look like people in magazines. (15) Men with careers in modeling or acting commonly have them. (16) A man with an eating disorder may also desire to be a better athlete. (17) Men suffering from bulimia and anorexia nervosa are often involved in sports that stress dieting. (18) Body builders are at high risk.

(19) Unfortunately, many men are unwilling to confess their problems. (20) In fact, many health professionals don't expect to see men with eating disorders. (21) They may misdiagnose men suffering from bulimia or anorexia. (22) Since eating disorder treatment programs were designed mainly for women. (23) Men may feel uncomfortable in that environment. (24) If a man can commit to a well-run, effective program he will most likely recover successfully.

(25) The American public seems preoccupies with weight loss nowadays. (26) It is no wonder that eating disorders are becoming more common in both men and women. (27) As long as these societal pressures exist, we can expect the number of cases to continue to rise. (28) Researchers are still learning how best to diagnose and treat men with these diseases.

1. Choose the word or phrase that **best** fits at the beginning of sentence 21.

    a. For example,
    b. Therefore,
    c. In fact,
    d. However,

2. Choose the correct way to write the underlined part of sentence 7.

    "Bulimia" involves rapidly eating lots of food and <u>than vomiting it up to prevent weight gain.</u>

    a. than vomiting it up to prevent wait gain.
    b. then vomiting it up to prevent weight gain.
    c. than vomiting it up, to prevent weight gain.
    d. No change is needed.

3. Which of these is **not** a complete sentence?

    a. In fact, as many as one million men suffer from eating disorders.
    b. Symptoms of this disorder include nervousness combined with lose of appetite.
    c. Since eating disorder treatment programs were designed mainly for women.
    d. Researchers are still learning how best to diagnose and treat men with these diseases.

4. Read sentence 3, which is poorly written.

    Some of these same disorders now affect men in the United States, such as anorexia nervosa and bulimia.

    Choose the **best** way to rewrite this sentence.

    a. Some of these same disorders, such as anorexia nervosa and bulimia, now affect men in the United States.
    b. Such as anorexia nervosa and bulimia, some of these same disorders now affect men in the United States.
    c. In the United States, some of these same disorders now affect men in the United States.
    d. Some of these same disorders now affect men, such as anorexia nervosa and bulimia, in the United States.

5. Choose the correct way to write the underlined part of sentence 25.

   The American <u>public seems preoccupies</u> with weight loss nowadays.

   a. Public seems preoccupies
   b. public seems preoccupied
   c. public seemed preoccupies
   d. No change is needed.

6. Choose the correct way to write the underlined part of sentence 11.

   They are also usually <u>anxious about food, and weight.</u>

   a. anxious about food, and, weight.
   b. anscious about food, and weight.
   c. anxious about food and weight.
   d. No change is needed.

7. Pete wants to add this sentence to the paragraph that begins with sentence 19.

   All-male support groups do exist.

   Where would the sentence **best** fit?

   a. right after sentence 19
   b. right after sentence 20
   c. right after sentence 21
   d. right after sentence 23

8. Choose the correct way to write the underlined part of sentence 9.

   Symptoms of this disorder <u>include nervousness combined with lose</u> of appetite.

   a. include nervousness combined with loss
   b. include nervousness combined, with lose
   c. includes nervousness combined with lose
   d. No change is needed.

9. Choose the correct way to write the underlined part of sentence 24.

If a man can commit to <u>a well-run, effective program he will</u> most likely recover successfully.

    a.   a well-run, efective program he will
    b.   a well-run, effective program, he will
    c.   a good-run, effective program he will
    d.   No change is needed.

10. Pete wants to change sentence 17 so that it is more specific.

Men suffering from bulimia and anorexia nervosa are often involved in <u>sports that stress dieting.</u>

Choose the **best** way to rewrite the underlined part of this sentence.

    a.   sports, which stress dieting.
    b.   sports where dieting is important.
    c.   all kinds of sports that stress dieting.
    d.   wrestling, running, and other sports that stress dieting.

June's social studies class has been studying Asian countries. Her teacher asks each student to choose a country and to write a report highlighting a particular issue that affects the country. June does some research at the local library and writes her rough draft. She needs your help editing and revising it.

Here is June's rough draft. Read it and then answer questions 1–10.

(1) Borneo, located southeast of the Malay Peninsula and southwest of the Philippines, is a mountainous Malaysian island. (2) It is the third largest island in the world. (3) Borneo's climate is hot and wet; portions of the island receive as much as 150–200 inches of rainfall each year. (4) Monsoons are not uncommon throughout the fall and winter seasons. (5) With all this rain, Borneo has one of the diversest collections of plants in the world. (6) Rainforests grow densely in certain areas.

(7) Over time, Borneo has been home to many different groups. (8) Native tribes still inhabit the island. (9) European explorers and traders began coming during the sixteenth century. (10) Today, the population is a diverse mix of native people, Asians, and europeans. (11) One group in particular, however, is currently threatened by extinction. (12) They are the Penan, who make there home in the state of Sarawak.

(13) Native tribes in Borneo rely heavily on the rainforest for their survival. (14) They live on the plants and animals. (15) Nearly all of Sarawak was once covered in forest. (16) More than half of it is licensed for logging. (17) Only about twelve percent of the rainforest has been protected and set aside for national parks and wildlife sanctuaries. (18) As of 1999, seventy percent of the rainforest in Sarawak had been stripped bare. (19) Logging, poaching, and man-made fires in the rainforests in Borneo caused problems for many animals. (20) The population of the red-haired orangutan found only in Borneo dropped from 180,000 to 30,000 in just ten years. (21) It now faces extinction. (22) Sarawak's state bird, the hornbill is also endangered. (23) Many plants did not survive the destructive logging practices. (24) The rivers have been polluted as well.

(25) The peaceable Penan nomads are mainly "animists, who believe that nature has a soul and forest spirits must be protected and left undisturbed. (26) They are one of the few hunter-gatherer tribes left in the world today. (27) Just about 260 native Penans were still living in the jungle in 1999, and the logging population largely outnumbered the 260 native Penans. (28) Of the 9,000 Penans in Borneo at that time, most had moved to government settlements, leaving only 63 families left to live in the rainforest. (29) These government settlements were largely described as hot, stifling refugee camps with dirty water.

(30) Like the rainforest, the native Penan way of life has been largely infiltrated and destroyed. (31) Western society has slowly crept into Borneo. (32) McDonald's restaurants and cell phones have popped up even on this remote island. (33) Sarawak has become a popular tourist destination. (34) Some remember a quiet, peaceful way of life in the rainforest. (35) One can only hope that them can soon return home.

1. Choose the sentence that could **best** be added right after sentence 17.

   a. Penan tribespeople use poison blowpipes and spears to protect themselves.
   b. The capital of Sarawak is Kuching.
   c. Even these areas, according to environmentalists, are threatened by erosion and river silt.
   d. Sarawak is the size of Mississippi.

2. Choose the correct way to write the underlined part of sentence 25.

   The peaceable Penan nomads are mainly "animists, who believe that nature has a soul and forest spirits must be protected and left undisturbed.

   a. The piecable Penan nomads are mainly "animists,
   b. The peaceable Penan nomads are mainly "animists,"
   c. The peaceable Penan nomads, are mainly "animists,
   d. No change is needed.

3. Choose the correct way to write the underlined part of sentence 5.

   With all this rain, Borneo has one of the diversest collections of plants in the world.

   a. of the most diverse collections of plants in the world.
   b. of the diversest collections of plants in the World.
   c. of the diversest, collections of plants in the world.
   d. No change is needed.

4. The topic sentence of the paragraph that begins with sentence 7 is

   a. sentence 7.
   b. sentence 9.
   c. sentence 10.
   d. sentence 12.

5. Choose the correct way to write the underlined part of sentence 35.

   One can only hope that <u>them can soon return home.</u>

   a. them can soon return home?
   b. them can soon return homes.
   c. they can soon return home.
   d. No change is needed.

6. Choose the correct way to write the underlined part of sentence 10.

   Today, the population is a diverse <u>mix of native people, Asians, and europeans.</u>

   a. mix of native people, Asians and europeans.
   b. mix of native people, Asians, and Europeans.
   c. mix, of native people, Asians, and europeans.
   d. No change is needed.

7. Read sentence 20, which is poorly written.

   The population of the red-haired orangutan found only in Borneo dropped from 180,000 to 30,000 in just ten years.

   Choose the **best** way to rewrite this sentence.

   a. From 180,000 to 30,000, in just ten years, the population of the red-haired orangutan found only in Borneo dropped.
   b. Borneo dropped its ten-year population of the red-haired orangutan from 180,000 to 30,000.
   c. Found only in Borneo, the ten red-haired orangutan population dropped from 180,000 to 30,000 in just ten years.
   d. The population of the red-haired orangutan, found only in Borneo, dropped from 180,000 to 30,000 in just ten years.

8. Choose the correct way to write the underlined part of sentence 22.

Sarawak's state <u>bird, the hornbill is also endangered.</u>

a. bird, the hornbill is, also endangered.
b. bird, the hornbill, is also endangered.
c. bird, the hornbill is also indangered.
d. No change is needed.

9. Choose the correct way to write the underlined part of sentence 12.

They are the Penan, who make <u>there home in the state of Sarawak.</u>

a. their home in the state of Sarawak.
b. there home in the State of Sarawak.
c. there home in the state of sarawak.
d. No change is needed.

10. Read sentence 27, which is poorly written.

Just about 260 native Penans were still living in the jungle in 1999, and the logging population largely outnumbered the 260 native Penans.

Choose the **best** way to rewrite this sentence.

a. Just about 260 native Penans were still living in the jungle in 1999, and the logging population, of about 260, outnumbered them.
b. In 1999, about 260 native Penans were still living in the jungle, and the logging population largely outnumbered the Penans.
c. The logging population largely outnumbered the approximately 260 native Penans still living in the jungle in 1999.
d. About 260 native Penans outnumbered the logging population in 1999, largely still living in the jungle.

Stanley's computer class has been studying recent advances in technology. His teacher asks the class to write reports discussing how a current trend is affecting teenagers. Stanley chooses his topic and writes his rough draft. He needs your help editing and revising it.

Here is Stanley's rough draft. Read it and then answer questions 1–10.

(1) If your like me, you probably have a blog. (2) If you're not familiar with the term, then let me explain it to you. (3) "Blog" is an abbreviation for "weblog," an expression coined by Jorn Barger, the owner of the long-established Robot Wisdom weblog. (4) A blog is basically an online diary. (5) In the past ten years or so, blogging has become one of the more trendy ways to comunicate over the Internet. (6) Teenagers aged thirteen to nineteen make up more than half of the bloggers in the United States. (7) It's a fun activity and fairly harmless, as long as you take the proper precautions.

(8) Keeping a blog allows you to express yourself in a new way. (9) You can be as honest and personal as you like, depending on what you want to include in your blog. (10) Many teenagers use blogs as a way to talk to each other about things in their lives. (11) Blogs are a great way to connect with others. (12) In fact, some teachers are now using blogs as a way to get their students to react to one anothers' work. (13) Teenagers use blogging today like teenagers in the 1980s used the mall—as a place to hang out!

(14) *The Mercury News* in San Jose California, did an extensive article on blogging. (15) Reporter K. Oanh Ha told of a fifteen-year-old freshman girl who learned everything she could about a classmate from his blog. (16) She never spoke with him face to face. (17) In fact, she was horrified by the notion. (18) She said "I read his [blog] every day and learned a lot about him." (19) She was able to determine that he was "too weird" after a few months and the two never even spoke. (20) Now I call that a cyber-crush?

(21) Blogs aren't difficult to figure out, either. (22) It is inexpensive to get started, and there is special software that makes blogging easy. (23) All you really needs is an Internet connection, the software, and the dedication to keep your blog going over time.

(24) Nevertheless, you should use caution when posting your information in a blog. (25) Don't tell weirdos where you're at or what you're into. (26) I'm sure you've heard of cyber-stalking and predation. (27) Its important that you don't expose yourself to dangerous characters looking to take advantage of you.

(28) Happy blogging!

1. Choose the correct way to write the underlined part of sentence 23.

   All you really needs is an Internet connection, the software, and the dedication to keep your blog going over time.

   a. All you really needs is an Internet Connection,
   b. All you really need is an Internet connection,
   c. All your really needs is an Internet connection,
   d. No change is needed.

2. Choose the correct way to write the underlined part of sentence 14.

   ***The Mercury News* in San Jose California, did an extensive article on blogging.**

   a. *The Mercury News* in San Jose, California, did an
   b. *The Mercury News* in San Jose California did an
   c. *The mercury news* in San Jose California, did an
   d. No change is needed.

3. Choose the correct way to write the underlined part of sentence 5.

   In the past ten years or so, blogging has become one of the more trendy ways to comunicate over the Internet.

   a. more trendie ways to comunicate over the Internet.
   b. more trendy ways to comunicate over the internet.
   c. more trendy ways to communicate over the Internet.
   d. No change is needed.

4. Choose the correct way to write the underlined part of sentence 20.

   Now I call that a cyber-crush?

   a. call that an cyber-crush?
   b. call that a cyber-crush!
   c. calling that a cyber-crush?
   d. No change is needed.

5. Choose the **best** way to write the underlined part of sentence 25 so that the composition maintains a consistent tone.

   Don't tell <u>weirdos where you're at or what you're into.</u>

   a. too many details about your location or other personal matters to strangers.
   b. strangers important info over the Internet; don't say I didn't warn you!
   c. strangers stuff about you, and watch out.
   d. people where you are and what you like to do; they're strangers.

6. Choose the correct way to write the underlined part of sentence 21.

   <u>Blogs aren't difficult to</u> figure out, either.

   a. Blogs aren't difficultest to
   b. Blogs wasn't difficult to
   c. Blogs aren't difficult too
   d. No change is needed.

7. Choose the correct way to write the underlined part of sentence 1.

   <u>If your like me,</u> you probably have a blog.

   a. If you like me,
   b. If your like me
   c. If you're like me,
   d. No change is needed.

8. Choose the correct way to write the underlined part of sentence 18.

   <u>She said "I read his [blog] every day</u> and learned a lot about him."

   a. She said, "I read his [blog] every day
   b. She said "I read him [blog] every day
   c. She said I read his [blog] every day
   d. No change is needed.

9. Stanley wants to change sentence 10 so that it is more specific.

    Many teenagers use blogs <u>as a way to talk to each other about things in their lives.</u>

    Choose the **best** way to rewrite the underlined part of this sentence.

    a. to talk to each other about all kinds of stuff.
    b. to talk to each other about things in their lives.
    c. as a way to communicate with each other on common topics.
    d. as a way to discuss issues at home, at school, or with friends.

10. Choose the correct way to write the underlined part of sentence 12.

    In fact, some teachers are now using blogs as a way to get <u>their students to react to one anothers' work.</u>

    a. their students to react too one anothers' work.
    b. their students to react to one another's work.
    c. there students to react to one anothers' work.
    d. No change is needed.

The principal of a Florida middle school has asked each student in the seventh grade to write a brief report about a place he or she visited on a field trip in the past school year. The principal is trying to determine where she will take the next class of seventh graders. Juniper chooses to write about the Coral Castle in Homestead. She has written her rough draft and needs your help editing and revising it.

Here is Juniper's rough draft. Read it and then answer questions 1–10.

(1) Edward Leedskalnin was born in Riga, Latvia, on August 10 1887. (2) At the age of 26, he was engaged to a sixteen-year-old named Agnes Scuffs, whom he called his "Sweet Sixteen." (3) She has been described as Leedskalnin's one true love. (4) Just a day before the wedding was to be held, Scuffs cancelled the ceremony breaking Leedskalnin's heart. (5) In memory of his lost love, this private man created one of the world's most remarkable accomplishments: the Coral Castle.

(6) How did the Egyptians move the gigantic stones to create the pyramids? (7) That is a mistory. (8) A similar mystery surrounds the building of Coral Castle in Homestead Florida. (9) It is believed that Leedskalnin single-handedly carved and sculpted over 1,100 tons of coral rock. (10) At just five feet tall and weighing merely 100 pounds, this small man somehow cut and moved these immense coral blocks using only hand tools. (11) Prior knowledge from working in lumber camps and in stone masonry helped him to know how to move them.

(12) Or did it? (13) Some people believe that he somehow learned the power harnessed by the Egyptians many years ago. (14) They think that he levitated the coral blocks. (15) Leedskalnin himself was quoted as saying, "I have discovered the secrets of the pyramids, and have found out how the Egyptians, . . . with only primitive tools, raised and set in place blocks of stone weighing many tons".

(16) Leedskalnin worked at night on his ten-acre plot in southern Florida. (17) Just how he managed to move these coral blocks, some of which weighed as much as 30 tons each, has not yet been discovered. (18) It is said that if he felt himself being watched at his work, he would quit what he was doing.

(19) Leedskalnin did not just build a castle structure with walls constructed of 15-ton blocks. (20) He erected a 22-ton obelisk, a three-ton rocking chair, numerous giant puzzles, and sculptures featuring planets and the moon. (21) A 30-ton telescope towers 25 feet above the complex. (22) It is perfectly aligned to the north star. (23) A working sundial accurately tells time within two minutes. (24) A 5,000-pound heart-shaped coral rock table is believed to be the largest valentine in the world. (25) Perhaps his most miraculous creation was a nine-ton gate that provides entrance to the castle. (26) The gate is 80 inches wide. (27) It is 92 inches tall. (28) It is 21 inches thick. (29) It is so perfectly balanced on its center of gravity that a person can open it by pushing with just one finger. (30) Incredible!

(continued on next page)

(continued from previous page)

(31) It is interesting to note that the area where Coral Castle can be found in is considered part of the Bermuda Triangle. (32) Leedskalnin has been described as highly intuitive and looked for signs of anomaly in nature. (33) His notebooks were filled with drawings and plans for magnetism and electrical experiments. (34) Although he had just a fourth-grade education, he is believed to perhaps have discovered a way to reduce the earth's gravitational pull. (35) Is this possible? (36) Until the mystery surrounding Coral Castle's construction is solved, we will never know.

(37) In December 1951, Leedskalnin became ill. (38) He put a sign on his door that said, "going to the Hospital," and took the bus to Jackson Memorial Hospital in Miami. (39) He died three days later in his sleep at the age of 64. (40) It took Ed Leedskalnin 28 years to build this testament of his love for Agnes Scuffs. (41) His spectacular accomplishment will continue to amaze visitors for years to come.

1. Choose the correct way to write the underlined part of sentence 15.

   Leedskalnin himself was quoted as saying, "I have discovered the secrets of the pyramids, and have found out how the Egyptians, . . . with only primitive tools, raised and <u>set in place blocks of stone weighing many tons</u>".

   a. sets in place blocks of stone weighing many tons".
   b. set in place blocks of stone weighing much tons".
   c. set in place blocks of stone weighing many tons."
   d. No change is needed.

2. Choose the **best** way to combine the ideas in sentences 26, 27, and 28 into one sentence.

   The gate is 80 inches wide. It is 92 inches tall. It is 21 inches thick.

   a. The gate is 80 inches wide, 92 inches tall, and 21 inches thick.
   b. The gate is 80, 90, and 21 inches wide, tall, and thick.
   c. The gate, which is 80 inches wide, is 92 inches tall and 21 inches thick.
   d. At 80 inches wide, 92 inches tall, and 21 inches wide is the gate.

3. Choose the correct way to write the underlined part of sentence 4.

Just a day before the wedding was to be held, <u>Scuffs cancelled the ceremony breaking Leedskalnin's heart.</u>

  a. Scuffs cancelled the ceremony, breaking Leedskalnin's heart.
  b. Scuffs canceled the ceremony breaking Leedskalnin's heart.
  c. Scuffs's cancelled the ceremony breaking Leedskalnin's heart.
  d. No change is needed.

4. Choose the correct way to write the underlined part of sentence 22.

It is perfectly <u>aligned to the north star.</u>

  a. alined to the north star.
  b. aligned to the North Star.
  c. aligned, to the north star.
  d. No change is needed.

5. Read sentence 32, which is poorly written.

Leedskalnin has been described as highly intuitive and looked for signs of anomaly in nature.

Choose the **best** way to rewrite this sentence.

  a. Leedskalnin looked for signs of anomaly in nature while being a highly intuitive man.
  b. Leedskalnin was both a highly intuitive man and someone who looked for signs of anomaly in nature.
  c. Leedskalnin has been described as a highly intuitive man who looked for signs of anomaly in nature.
  d. Leedskalnin's highly intuitive nature helped him look for signs of anomaly.

6. Choose the correct way to write the underlined part of sentence 7.

That is <u>a mistory.</u>

    a. an mistory.
    b. a mistory?
    c. a mystery.
    d. No change is needed.

7. Choose the correct way to write the underlined part of sentence 38.

He put a sign on his door that <u>said, "going to the Hospital," and took the bus</u> to Jackson Memorial Hospital in Miami.

    a. said, "Going to the Hospital," and took the bus
    b. said, "going to the Hospital," and had taken the bus
    c. said "going to the Hospital," and took the bus
    d. No change is needed.

8. Read sentence 19, which is poorly written.

Leedskalnin did not just build a castle structure with walls constructed of 15-ton blocks.

Choose the **best** way to rewrite this sentence.

    a. Leedskalnin did not just build a castle structure with constructed walls of 15-ton blocks.
    b. Leedskalnin built a 15-ton castle structure with walls of 15-ton blocks.
    c. Leedskalnin not just built a castle with walls constructed of 15-ton blocks.
    d. Leedskalnin did not just construct a castle with walls of 15-ton blocks.

9. Choose the correct way to write the underlined part of sentence 1.

Edward Leedskalnin was born <u>in Riga, Latvia, on August 10 1887.</u>

a. in riga, Latvia, on August 10 1887.
b. in Riga, Latvia, on August 10, 1887.
c. in Riga Latvia, on August 10 1887.
d. No change is needed.

10. Read sentence 31, which is poorly written.

It is interesting to note that the area where Coral Castle can be found in is considered part of the Bermuda Triangle.

Choose the **best** way to rewrite this sentence.

a. Coral Castle can, interestingly enough, be found in a considered part of the Bermuda Triangle.
b. Finding the Bermuda Triangle within Coral Castle is an interesting consideration, in part, to note.
c. Interestingly, the area where Coral Castle can be found is considered part of the Bermuda Triangle.
d. Noting that the area where Coral Castle can be found is considered part of the Bermuda Triangle is interesting.

Shane's seventh-grade health class has been studying fitness. His teacher has asked that each student write a report on a topic related to fitness and exercise. Shane chooses his topic, visits the library, and writes his rough draft. He needs your help editing and revising it.

Here is Shane's rough draft. Read it and then answer questions 1–10.

---

(1) Many runners thinking that they are preventing injury, stretch their muscles before heading out to run. (2) However, new research shows that some runners get hurt more because they stretch. (3) A study conducted by Dr. David A. Lally of the University of Hawaii at manoa backs this idea.

(4) Dr. Lally surveyed 1,543 runners participating in the Honolulu Marathon. (5) He found that high-mileage runners and those who worked out for long periods of time were more likely to be injured. (6) While low-mileage, short-duration runners less likely. (7) (An injury in this case is damage done to the body that would prohibit usual training for at least five days). (8) Perhaps these findings are not that surprising. (9) However, what may be more surprising is Dr. Lally's discovery that stretching is also linked with more injuries.

(10) Dr. Lally's survey found that 47 percent of the male runners who regularly stretched were hurt during the past year. (11) This percentage was made up entirely of white men. (12) Of those who didn't stretch, only 33 percent suffered an injury. (13) In women, however, Dr. Lally found that those who stretched had the same rate of injury as those women who did not. (14) Of the Asians included in the survey, the amount of stretching affected neither men nor women.

(15) When interviewed by *Peak Performance* magazine, Dr. Lally could not explain why stretching and injuries in white males should be so closely related. (16) He said, "but there's certainly no . . . reason why stretching should limit injury risk. (17) After all, most running injuries are caused by overuse, and stretching your muscles before workouts is not going to prevent you from overusing them.

(18) The time when the stretches are done could factor in. (19) Those runners who stretched after they ran instead of before had fewer of injuries when compared to those who didn't stretch at all. (20) Muscles are usually fairly tight when you finish exercising. (21) Stretching at the end of a workout could relax the fibers in the muscles. (22) You will then be better prepared for regular daily activities.

(23) Dr. Lallys' survey provides an intriguing view for runners. (24) Of course, every person's body is different and each athlete should make an educated decision regarding his or her best stretching routine. (25) Next time you go out for a run, think about what your body might be trying to tell you.

1. Choose the word or phrase that **best** fits at the beginning of sentence 21.

    a. For example,
    b. Therefore,
    c. Next,
    d. In other words,

2. Choose the correct way to write the underlined part of sentence 3.

    A study conducted by Dr. David A. Lally of the University of Hawaii <u>at manoa backs this idea.</u>

    a. at Manoa backs this idea.
    b. at manoa back this idea.
    c. at manoa backs this ideas.
    d. No change is needed.

3. Choose the correct way to write the underlined part of sentence 23.

    <u>Dr. Lallys' survey provides an intriguing</u> view for runners.

    a. Dr. Lallys' survey provides an intreeging
    b. Dr. Lallys' survey provide an intriguing
    c. Dr. Lally's survey provides an intriguing
    d. No change is needed.

4. Choose the sentence that could **best** be added right after sentence 14.

    a. Dr. Lally's survey was filled with inconclusive data.
    b. Men and women of all races were found to have the same rate of injury if they stretched before running the marathon.
    c. Asians refused to stretch, which explains why they were not included in the survey.
    d. Overall, Dr. Lally found the highest connection between stretching and injury in white males.

5. Choose the correct way to write the underlined part of sentence 17.

After all, most running injuries are caused by overuse, and stretching your muscles before workouts is not going to <u>prevent you from overusing them.</u>

   a. prevent you from overusing them."
   b. prevent you from overuseing them.
   c. prevent you're overusing them.
   d. No change is needed.

6. Which of these is **not** a complete sentence?

   a. While low-mileage, short-duration runners less likely.
   b. Perhaps these findings are not that surprising.
   c. Muscles are usually fairly tight when you finish exercising.
   d. Of course, every person's body is different and each athlete should make an educated decision regarding his or her best stretching routine.

7. Read sentence 9, which is poorly written.

However, what may be more surprising is Dr. Lally's discovery that stretching is also linked with more injuries.

Choose the **best** way to rewrite this sentence.

   a. What may be more surprising is that Dr. Lally discovered that stretching is also linked with more injuries.
   b. What Dr. Lally discovered may be more surprising, however, when it pertains to injuries and stretching.
   c. More surprising is Dr. Lally's discovery linking higher amounts of stretching with a higher frequency of injuries.
   d. Injuries and stretching may be linked by Dr. Lally's more surprising discovery.

8. Choose the correct way to write the underlined part of sentence 1.

   Many runners thinking that they are preventing injury, stretch their muscles before heading out to run.

   a. Many runners thinking that, they are preventing injury,
   b. Many runners, thinking that they are preventing injury,
   c. Many runners thinking that they are prevents injury,
   d. No change is needed.

9. Choose the correct way to write the underlined part of sentence 7.

   (An injury in this case is damage done to the body that would prohibit usual training for at least five days).

   a. trayning for at least five days).
   b. training for at least five days.)
   c. training for, at least five days).
   d. No change is needed.

10. Choose the correct way to write the underlined part of sentence 16.

    He said, "but there's certainly no . . . reason why stretching should limit injury risk.

    a. "but theirs certainly
    b. "but, there's certainly
    c. "But there's certainly
    d. No change is needed.

Alaya's seventh-grade science class is studying reptiles and amphibians. Her teacher has asked each student to write a report about one reptile or amphibian. Alaya does her research and writes her rough draft. She needs your help editing and revising it.

Here is Alaya's rough draft. Read it and then answer questions 1–10.

(1) In a cave deep in a partially destroyed forest in jaragua national park, the smallest living lizard species lay hidden. (2) It wasn't until 2001 that biologists discovered it. (3) The Jaragua Sphaero, or dwarf gecko, is the world's smallest lizard among 23,000 known species of birds, mammals, and reptiles.

(4) The scientific name of the dwarf gecko, *Sphaerodactylus ariasae*, is named after Yvonne Arias. (5) She was head of the Dominican conservation organization, Grupo Jaragua. (6) Blair Hedges of Pennsylvania State University and Richard Thomas of the University of Puerto Rico, found this new species within the national park on Beata Island, which is in the Dominican Republic. (7) The dwarf gecko measures just two centimeters from nose to tail and weighs a mere .00455 ounces. (8) It comfortably fits on a U.S. dime. (9) Dr. Hedges said that finding the gecko was a surprising discovery. (10) He was reminded that us do not know everything about the Earth around us. (11) In an area heavily studied for hundreds of years, it is amazing and wonderful that new species can still be found.

(12) The Caribbean Islands feature both the smallest and largest of some other species as well. (13) There are fewer species to compete with, so these unique birds, mammals, and reptiles appear. (14) The world's smallest bird, the Bee Hummingbird is merely five centimeters long. (15) It is found only in Cuba. (16) A frog measured just one centimeter can also be found in Cuba. (17) The West Indies feature the world's smallest snake, the Lesser Antillean Threadsnake. (18) This snake could make it's way through the path left in a pencil if the lead were removed.

(19) While the Caribbean is one of the best places on the planet to find unique species, overpopulation and logging practices threaten that natchural environment. (20) Immediately upon being found, the dwarf gecko was declared an endangered species. (21) It makes I wonder how many other species have come and gone without ever having been discovered.

1. Choose the correct way to write the underlined part of sentence 21.

   It makes I wonder how many other species have come and gone without ever having been discovered.

   a. It makes me wonder how many other species
   b. It makes I wonder how much other species
   c. It made I wonder how many other species
   d. No change is needed.

2. Choose the correct way to write the underlined part of sentence 1.

In a cave deep in <u>a partially destroyed forest in jaragua national park,</u> the smallest living lizard species lay hidden.

a. a partially destroy forest in jaragua national park,
b. a partially, destroyed forest in jaragua national park,
c. a partially destroyed forest in Jaragua National Park,
d. No change is needed.

3. Choose the correct way to write the underlined part of sentence 6.

Blair Hedges of Pennsylvania State University and Richard Thomas <u>of the University of Puerto Rico, found this new species</u> within the national park on Beata Island, which is in the Dominican Republic.

a. of the University of Puerto Rico, found this new speceis
b. of the University of Puerto Rico found this new species
c. of the University of Puerto Rico and found this new species
d. No change is needed.

4. Read sentence 4, which is poorly written.

The scientific name of the dwarf gecko, *Sphaerodactylus ariasae*, is named after Yvonne Arias.

Choose the **best** way to rewrite this sentence.

a. The scientific name of the dwarf gecko, *Sphaerodactylus ariasae*, comes from Yvonne Arias.
b. *Sphaerodactylus ariasae*, the scientific name of the dwarf gecko, is just like Yvonne Arias's name.
c. The dwarf gecko's scientific name, *Sphaerodactylus ariasae*, refers to Yvonne Arias.
d. *Sphaerodactylus ariasae* is the dwarf gecko's scientific name, which is named after Yvonne Arias.

157

5. Choose the correct way to write the underlined part of sentence 19.

    While the Caribbean is one of the best places on the planet to find unique species, overpopulation and <u>logging practices threaten that natchural environment.</u>

    a. logging practices threaten that natural environment.
    b. loging practices threaten that natchural environment.
    c. logging practices threatening that natchural environment.
    d. No change is needed.

6. Choose the correct way to write the underlined part of sentence 10.

    <u>He was reminded that us do not know</u> everything about the Earth around us.

    a. He was remind that us do not know
    b. He was reminded that we do not know
    c. He was reminded that us do not no
    d. No change is needed.

7. Choose the correct way to write the underlined part of sentence 14.

    The world's smallest bird, <u>the Bee Hummingbird is merely</u> five centimeters long.

    a. the Bee Hummingbird is meerly
    b. the Bee Hummingbird, is merely
    c. the Bee Hummingbird are merely
    d. No change is needed.

158

8. Read sentence 13, which is poorly written.

    There are fewer species to compete with, so these unique birds, mammals, and reptiles appear.

    Choose the **best** way to rewrite this sentence.

    a. Species competing less makes more unique birds, mammals, and reptiles appear.
    b. With fewer species to compete with, unique birds, mammals, and reptiles appear.
    c. Fewer species competing means more appearing unique birds, mammals, and reptiles.
    d. There are fewer species with which to compete, so more unique birds, mammals, and reptiles appear.

9. Choose the correct way to write the underlined part of sentence 16.

    A <u>frog measured just one centimeter can also be</u> found in Cuba.

    a. frog measuring just one centimeter can also be
    b. frog measured just one centimeter, can also be
    c. frog measured just one centimeter could also been
    d. No change is needed.

10. Choose the correct way to write the underlined part of sentence 18.

    This snake could <u>make it's way through the path left in a pencil</u> if the lead were removed.

    a. make it's weigh through the path left in a pencil
    b. make its way through the path left in a pencil
    c. make it's way through the paths left in a pencil
    d. No change is needed.

Rick's seventh-grade social studies class has been studying trends in contemporary society. His teacher has asked each student to choose a trend from the past fifty years and write a report about it. Rick visits his local library and writes his rough draft. He needs your help editing and revising it.

Here is Rick's rough draft. Read it and then answer questions 1–10.

(1) The Coca-Cola company did an experiment on the North American soft-drink lover beginning on April 23, 1985. (2) Launching "New Coke" with the slogan, "The Best Just Got Better," the company ended the production of the much-loved original Coca-Cola product and replaced it with a new formula. (3) They made a mistake by not asking testing groups whether or not they would be interested in a new Coke product.

(4) What made Coke decide to launch New Coke! (5) Product testers found that more people preferred the sweeter taste of Pepsi. (6) The two companies had been competing for customers for many years. (7) Coca-Cola's popularity had been shrinking since World War II. (8) In fact, the only thing keeping Coke afloat was that it was available in more vending machines and fast-food restaurants. (9) Newer products were making the market tougher on cola sales. (10) These other beverages included those manufactured by the Coca-Cola and Pepsi companies.

(11) Diet Coke was first released in 1982. (12) It became an instant success with its smoother flavor. (13) In fact, Diet Coke's taste was similarer to Pepsi than to the original formula for Coca-Cola. (14) By 1984, Diet Coke was number three among soft drinks in America. (15) Taste tests were held to determine if Coke or Pepsi was the preferred cola beverage among Americans. (16) People liked Pepsi better.

(17) New Coke was developed and tested and tasted smoother and sweeter than original Coke and was more like Pepsi. (18) Blind taste tests showed that people who tasted the experimental beverage claimed to like it better than original Coke or Pepsi. (19) It appeared that the Coca-Cola company had a winner. (20) The company decided to discontinue production of original Coke when they released New Coke.

(21) So what happened? (22) In blind taste tests, people had loved the new formula. (23) What the company didn't realize was that Coca-Cola's advertising campaign had successfully convinced the American public that original Coke was a central part of being American. (24) When the company released New Coke people who hadn't even tasted it (and those who had) said they hated it. (25) They disliked the taste. (26) They were also unhappy that them could no longer buy the original Coke product. (27) By not asking test subjects how they would feel if a new cola replaced the old one, the Coca-Cola company had made a huge mistake.

(28) On July 11, 1985, two Coca-Cola executives made an announcement: We have heard you." (29) People's attachment to the original Coke product was a factor they had not accounted for during all their endless tests and marketing analyses. (30) The

(continued on next page)

160

(continued from previous page)

company re-released the original formula as Coca-Cola Classic, or Classic Coke. (31) The news was so big that Peter Jennings interrupted "General Hospital" to make the announcement on national television. (32) The demand for the product grows and Coke soon beat out Pepsi in the market.

(33) Some people believe that the Coca-Cola company knew all along that this "New Coke" idea would result in better sales in the long run. (34) Some think this is a foolish idea and believe that the company truly thought New Coke would be a success.

1. Choose the correct way to write the underlined part of sentence 24.

   When the <u>company released New Coke people</u> who hadn't even tasted it (and those who had) said they hated it.

   a. company released New Coke people's
   b. company released New Coke, people
   c. company releesed New Coke people
   d. No change is needed.

2. Choose the correct way to write the underlined part of sentence 13.

   In fact, Diet Coke's taste <u>was similarer to Pepsi than</u> to the original formula for Coca-Cola.

   a. was similarer to Pepsi then
   b. was similarer to Pepsi, than
   c. was more similar to Pepsi than
   d. No change is needed.

3. Choose the correct way to write the underlined part of sentence 26.

   They were also unhappy <u>that them could no longer buy</u> the original Coke product.

   a. that them could no longer, buy
   b. that they could no longer buy
   c. that them can no longer buy
   d. No change is needed.

4. Read sentence 17, which is poorly written.

New Coke was developed and tested and tasted smoother and sweeter than original Coke and was more like Pepsi.

Choose the **best** way to rewrite this sentence.

   a. New Coke was developed, tested, and found to taste smoother and sweeter than the original Coke. In fact, it was more like Pepsi.

   b. New Coke developed and tested a new smoother, sweeter taste that was more like Pepsi and less than the original Coke.

   c. New Coke was developed and tested and was more like Pepsi. It had a smoother, sweeter taste than original Coke.

   d. New Coke was more like Pepsi with its smoother sweeter taste. It was developed and tested more than the original Coke.

5. Choose the word or phrase that **best** fits at the beginning of sentence 3.

   a. For example,
   b. In fact,
   c. Moreover,
   d. However,

6. Choose the correct way to write the underlined part of sentence 32.

The demand for <u>the product grows and Coke soon</u> beat out Pepsi in the market.

   a. the product grew and Coke soon
   b. the product grow's and Coke soon
   c. the product grows and Coke, soon
   d. No change is needed.

7. Choose the correct way to write the underlined part of sentence 4.

What made Coke <u>decide to launch New Coke!</u>

   a. decide to lawnch New Coke!
   b. decides to launch New Coke!
   c. decide to launch New Coke?
   d. No change is needed.

8. Choose the **best** way to combine the ideas in sentences 9 and 10 into one sentence.

Newer products were making the market tougher on cola sales. These other beverages included those manufactured by the Coca-Cola and Pepsi companies.

   a. Newer products were making the market tougher on cola sales, whose other beverages included those manufactured by the Coca-Cola and Pepsi companies.
   b. The Coca-Cola and Pepsi companies were manufacturing other beverages that made the newer products on the market tougher on cola sales.
   c. The market was tougher on the Coca-Cola and Pepsi companies, who were making newer products that were tougher on cola sales.
   d. Newer products, including those manufactured by the Coca-Cola and Pepsi companies, were making the market tougher on cola sales.

9. Choose the correct way to write the underlined part of sentence 28.

On July 11, 1985, two Coca-Cola executives made an announcement: <u>We have heard you."</u>

   a. We have hear you."
   b. "We have heard you."
   c. We have heard you?"
   d. No change is needed.

10. Read sentence 29, which is poorly written.

People's attachment to the original Coke product was a factor they had not accounted for during all their endless tests and marketing analyses.

Choose the **best** way to rewrite this sentence.

a. People's attachment to the endless tests and marketing analyses could not account for the original Coke product.
b. People were attached to the original Coke product, but only after endless tests and marketing analyses.
c. Endless tests and marketing analyses did not account for people's attachment to the original Coke product.
d. The original Coke product was so much of a factor during all their endless tests and marketing analyses that they could not remember the people's attachment.

Reginald's seventh-grade social studies class has been studying different means of communicating. His teacher has asked each student to write a report about a form of communication. Reginald does some research and writes his rough draft. He needs your help editing and revising it.

Here is Reginald's rough draft. Read it and then answer questions 1–10.

(1) Jim Carlson, the head of the arts program in San Quentin California, made a unique decision; he wanted to take juggling to prisons. (2) He felt that juggling forced people to work together, while keeping a rhythm going. (3) When Sara Felder first moved to San Quentin, she worked with Carlson. (4) Felder enrolled in Carlson's juggling program.

(5) Carlson's program was soon underway. (6) The men Felder had volunteered to work with in the maximum-security prison in San Quentin were often pensive. (7) The facility was mostly populated with inmates who were serving life sentences. (8) While Felder admits to being frightened by the environment at first, she said she never felt unsafe with the inmates. (9) She treated them like human beings and, naturally, liked some more than others.

(10) By working together and being patient, the inmates seemed to take to juggling right away. (11) A man serving a life sentence learns pretty quickly that all he has left is time. (12) Few of these inmates appeared to grow impatient when they couldn't immediately learn a trick. (13) The men learned grace, flexibility, and beauty. (14) Meanwhile, Felder realizes that learning juggling was a positive experience for these men who, for much of their lives, had known failure and defeat. (15) Succeeding at juggling and trying something new was an exceedingly rewarding experience—for both the men and they're teacher. (16) The inmates worked very hard to get it right. (17) As Felder remembers it, they created "beauty in a pretty ugly place."

(18) The security at the facility in San Quentin was changed to minimum, which altered its atmosphere. (19) While Felder often found working with inmates in for life sentences to be very rewarding, she found that most inmates serving shorter periods of time were not interested in learning about juggling or working together. (20) Some would try it to pass the time or to teach it to their children when they were released. (21) It wasn't about being creative for these inmates; it was more of a hobby.

(22) Felder's next volunteer assignment was in vacaville in a maximum-security prison for the mentally and physically ill. (23) Felder described this prison as a "black hole . . . just desperate energy and it was all contained." (24) She said that since there was so much "crazy" activity, juggling just seemed to fit in. (25) Mentally ill patients who didn't seem to understand a word that was being said to them would calmly take objects and start juggling them. (26) Slowly, some of the inmates would grow proud of their accomplishments. (27) Juggling was a healthy means of communicating. (28) A way to keep their brains active.

(continued on next page)

(continued from previous page)

(29) As of 1996, Sara Felder was working at a halfway house in San Francisco. (30) The facility was for men and women who had recently been released from prison or who were on parole, some of whom were dealing with addictions. (31) She was teaching theater and clowning, which includes juggling. (32) The ex-convicts in her troupe performed for little kids. (33) These activities filled Felder with a growing sense of pride.

(34) While Sara Felder wasn't sure she still had it in her to return to teaching in prison, the benefits of learning from a diverse group of people had not completely evaporated. (35) She said, "I always learn a lot and I think I have something to give to them, but it might be someone else's turn to take it over. . . . (36) I think I paid a price. (37) Emotionally, physically, I think it was hard. . . . (38) I think for a lot of us, juggling has saved our lives".

1. Choose the correct way to write the underlined part of sentence 14.

    <u>Meanwhile, Felder realizes that learning juggling</u> was a positive experience for these men who, for much of their lives, had known failure and defeat.

    a. Meanwhile Felder realizes that learning juggling
    b. Meanwhile, Felder realized that learning juggling
    c. Meanwhile, Felder realizes that learning jugling
    d. No change is needed.

2. Which of these is **not** a complete sentence?

    a. The facility was mostly populated with inmates who were serving life sentences.
    b. Few of these inmates appeared to grow impatient when they couldn't immediately learn a trick.
    c. A way to keep their brains active.
    d. I think I paid a price.

3. Choose the correct way to write the underlined part of sentence 1.

    Jim Carlson, the head of <u>the arts program in San Quentin California,</u> made a unique decision; he wanted to take juggling to prisons.

    a. the arts' program in San Quentin California,
    b. the arts program in San Quentin, California,
    c. the arts program in San Quentin California
    d. No change is needed.

166

4. Choose the correct way to write the underlined part of sentence 34.

While Sara Felder wasn't sure she still had it in her to return to teaching in prison, <u>the benefits of learning from a diverse group of people</u> had not completely evaporated.

a. the benefits of learning from a diverss group of people
b. the benefits of learning from a diverse group of people,
c. the benefits of learning form a diverse group of people
d. No change is needed.

5. Read sentence 19, which is poorly written.

While Felder often found working with inmates in for life sentences to be very rewarding, she found that most inmates serving shorter periods of time were not interested in learning about juggling or working together.

Choose the **best** way to rewrite this sentence.

a. While working with inmates serving life sentences was very rewarding, Felder found that fewer of those serving shorter terms were interested in learning about juggling or working together.
b. Working with inmates serving life sentences was much like those serving shorter sentences because they were both interested in juggling and working together.
c. Felder thought that while inmates serving life sentences were very rewarding, those serving for shorter periods of time were learning juggling and working together.
d. Inmates serving for shorter periods of time were interested in learning juggling and working together, while those inmates serving life sentences were being rewarded.

6. Choose the correct way to write the underlined part of sentence 22.

Felder's next <u>volunteer assignment was in vacaville</u> in a maximum-security prison for the mentally and physically ill.

a. vollunteer assignment was in vacaville
b. volunteer assignment, was in vacaville
c. volunteer assignment was in Vacaville
d. No change is needed.

7. Choose the **best** way to combine the ideas in sentences 6 and 7 into one sentence.

    The men Felder had volunteered to work with in the maximum-security prison in San Quentin were often pensive. The facility was mostly populated with inmates who were serving life sentences.

    a. Felder volunteered to work with men in the maximum-security prison in San Quentin who were serving life sentences and pensive.
    b. In the maximum-security prison in San Quentin, the men who were serving life sentences in the prison, who Felder volunteered to work with, were pensive.
    c. The pensive men in the maximum-security prison in San Quentin, most of whom were serving life sentences, were the ones that Felder volunteered to work with.
    d. The men that Felder volunteered to work with in the maximum-security prison in San Quentin, most of whom were serving life sentences, were often pensive.

8. Choose the correct way to write the underlined part of sentence 15.

    Succeeding at juggling and trying something new was an exceedingly rewarding experience—for both the men and they're teacher.

    a. for both the men and their teacher.
    b. for both the men, and they're teacher.
    c. for both the men and they're teacher?
    d. No change is needed.

9. Choose the correct way to write the underlined part of sentence 38.

    I think for a lot of us, juggling has saved our lives".

    a. juggling has saved our lifes".
    b. juggling have saved our lives".
    c. juggling has saved our lives."
    d. No change is needed.

10. Choose the sentence that could **best** be added right after sentence 21.

    a. Felder really enjoyed working with these inmates much more.
    b. Felder found that teaching these inmates became a less than meaningful experience for her and for them.
    c. Teaching these inmates was a lot like teaching the men who were in for life sentences.
    d. The prison, don't forget, was in San Quentin, California.

Heloise's seventh-grade French class has been studying eighteenth-century French philosophers. Her teacher has asked the students in the class to write reports on one of the philosophers they have been discussing. Heloise visits the library, composes an outline, and writes her report. She needs your help editing and revising it.

Here is Heloise's rough draft. Read it and then answer questions 1–10.

(1) Jean-Jacques Rousseau, philosopher and author, has been called undisciplined. (2) He has also been called a brilliant, original thinker. (3) He is beyond a doubt one of the most controversial, forward-thinking philosophers of the eighteenth century.

(4) Rousseau was born in Geneva on June 28, 1712. (5) His mother died while giving birth to him, and his violent, depressed father deserted him when he was just sixteen years old. (6) Rousseau became an apprentice to a notary and then to a coppersmith. (7) In 1728, however, he ran away to escape the disciplined lifestyle. (8) After wandering for several days, priests in Savoy turned him, who sent him to a school, over to Madame de Warens. (9) He worked in several households before settling with Madame de Warens in Chambery in 1730. (10) He studied nature, mathematics, latin, and music. (11) He read English, German, and French philosophy and chemistry. (12) He became interested in opera and theater.

(13) Rousseau traveled to Paris where he wrote a failed opera called *Les Muses Galantes*. (14) He also copied music for a living and was a secretery to Madame Dupin. (15) He fathered several illegitimate children, but refused to support them. (16) While in his forties, he began working as an author.

(17) During the French revolution, Rousseau's writings were highly controversial. (18) He first attracted attention with the prize-winning essay, *Discourse on the Sciences and the Arts* published in 1750. (19) He thought modern civilization did more harm than good. (20) He described it as artificial and corrupt. (21) He thought that people would benefit more by returning back to nature. (22) He also claimed that pursuing the arts and sciences degraded people's morals. (23) He felt that error and prejudice smothered reason and nature.

(24) In 1762, he published *Émile, on education*. (25) He proposed a method of education that would be better for students. (26) The French parliament ordered that *Émile* should be burned and Rousseau should be arrested. (27) He fled to Prussia and then to the Isle St. Pierre. (28) When the government of the Isle St. Pierre ordered him out of the territory. (29) He moved in with another philosopher and author, David Hume, in England. (30) Rousseau had grown paranoid and suspicious. (31) He left England to return to France.

(32) Rousseau's 1755 *Discourse on the Origin and Foundation of Inequality Among Mankind* applied his theories to politics. (33) He felt that a lot of politicians and

(continued on next page)

(continued from previous page)

intellectuals had a messed up way of looking at things, so then a lot of other people suffered. (34) In 1762, he proposed *The Social Contract* as the solution to problems discussed in his *Discourse*. (35) He described his idea that all men are born free and equal. (36) He said that all citizens agree to be protected by a governing body. (37) However, they do not give up their basic rights to it.

(38) Rousseau wrote *Confessions*, an autobiography of his unstable life, which he wrote throughout his life. (39) It was published in 1783, five years after Rousseau died in Ermenonville.

1. Read sentence 38, which is poorly written.

   Rousseau wrote *Confessions*, an autobiography of his unstable life, which he wrote throughout his life.

   Choose the **best** way to rewrite this sentence.

   a. Rousseau wrote *Confessions* throughout his life, which was an autobiography of his unstable life.
   b. *Confessions*, an autobiography of his unstable life, was written throughout Rousseau's life.
   c. Rousseau's *Confessions*, throughout his life, was an autobiography of his unstable life.
   d. Throughout the years of his unstable life, Rousseau wrote an autobiography entitled *Confessions*.

2. Choose the correct way to write the underlined part of sentence 17.

   <u>During the French revolution,</u> Rousseau's writings were highly controversial.

   a. During the French Revolution,
   b. During the French revolution
   c. During the french revolution,
   d. No change is needed.

170

3. Heloise wants to add this sentence to the paragraph that begins with sentence 24.

   He even fought with his close friends because they would not make his enemies their enemies.

   Where would the sentence **best** fit?

   a. right after sentence 26
   b. right after sentence 28
   c. right after sentence 30
   d. right after sentences 31

4. Choose the correct way to write the underlined part of sentence 14.

   He also copied music for a living and <u>was a secretery to Madame Dupin.</u>

   a. was a secretery to madame Dupin.
   b. was a secretary to Madame Dupin.
   c. were a secretery to Madame Dupin.
   d. No change is needed.

5. Heloise wants to change sentence 25 so that it is more specific.

   He proposed a method of education <u>that would be better for students.</u>

   Choose the **best** way to rewrite the underlined part of this sentence.

   a. that would benefit the students.
   b. to explore and support students' strengths, rather than to hold them back.
   c. that would enhance the students' educational experience.
   d. would make things more exciting and interesting for the students.

6. Choose the correct way to write the underlined part of sentence 18.

He first attracted attention with the prize-winning essay, _Discourse on the Sciences and the Arts_ published in 1750.

   a. _discourse on the sciences and the arts_ published in 1750.
   b. _Discourse on the Sciences and the Arts_ published in 1750?
   c. _Discourse on the Sciences and the Arts_, published in 1750.
   d. No change is needed.

7. Which of these is **not** a complete sentence?

   a. He worked in several households before settling with Madame de Warens in Chambery in 1730.
   b. He fathered several illegitimate children, but refused to support them.
   c. When the government of the Isle St. Pierre ordered him out of the territory.
   d. It was published in 1783, five years after Rousseau died in Ermenonville.

8. Choose the correct way to write the underlined part of sentence 10.

He studied nature, mathematics, latin, and music.

   a. nature, mathematics, Latin, and music.
   b. nature, mathematics, latin, and music?
   c. nature, mathmatics, latin, and music
   d. No change is needed.

172

9. Read sentence 8, which is poorly written.

    After wandering for several days, priests in Savoy turned him, who sent him to a school, over to Madame de Warens.

    Choose the **best** way to rewrite this sentence.

    a. After wandering for several days, Madame de Warens and the priests in Savoy turned him over to a school.
    b. After wandering for several days, priests in Savoy turned him over to Madame de Warens, who sent him to a school.
    c. Priests in Savoy, who found him wandering after several days, turned him over to Madame de Warens, who sent him to a school.
    d. Madame de Warens sent him to a school, while priests in Savoy wandered for several days.

10. Choose the **best** way to write the underlined part of sentence 33 so that the composition maintains a consistent tone.

    He felt that a lot of politicians and intellectuals had a messed up way of looking at things, so then a lot of other people suffered.

    a. politicians and intellectuals didn't have a clue when it came to what was good for other people.
    b. many politicians and intellectuals were bad.
    c. people suffered because politicians and intellectuals were a mess.
    d. flawed political and intellectual thinking caused most of the human injustice in the world.

173

Manuel has been asked by his seventh-grade history teacher to write a report about an event or practice in the United States that conflicts with the following statement by Dwight D. Eisenhower: "[We should] not try to conceal the thinking of our own people. They are part of America. And even if they think ideas that are contrary to ours, their right to say them, their right to record them, and their right to have them at places where they're accessible to others is unquestioned, or it's not America." Manuel maps out a web of ideas and writes his rough draft. He needs your help editing and revising it.

Here is Manuel's rough draft. Read it and then answer questions 1–10.

(1) Imagine that your at your local library perusing the fiction shelves. (2) Your eye wanders over the brightly-colored spines. (3) Suddenly, you start to notice that some of the books are disappearing. (4) The time-honored favorites that you've enjoyed reading are beginning to fade away. (5) Could this really happen.

(6) The short answer is yes. (7) Censorship in the United States has long been a problem. (8) When it affects you and your freedoms, it's your responsibility to speak up. (9) Librarians do their fair share of fighting against special interest groups who target so-called indecent literature. (10) To be truly effective, we must all take part in the battle for the freedom to read what we chose. (11) Our First Amendment rights of free speech and free press are violated every time a book is challenged or banned. (12) Protect your rights!

(13) Living in America grants us another freedom: the freedom of information. (14) We are at liberty to access information from almost anywhere. (15) Some of the books with controversial or disturbing subjects have been banned or challenged for their presentation of these subjects. (16) People deserve to be given the choice to disregard or take note of any information that they encounter.

(17) Today, kids seem to spend so much time in front of the television or on the computer. (18) Reading is a healthy, stimulating activity that should be fostered, not smothered. (19) Strengthening the family bond through reading, books bring adults and children together as well. (20) Some topics are just not easy to discuss with others. (21) Often, after reading about an awkward subject in a book, a child will feel more comfortable discussing it with a friend or family member. (22) Censors seek to protect children by warding off what they perceive as harmful to others, thereby taking away their right to decide for themselves.

(23) Just as each one of us has the right to express him- or herself, censors share the same freedom. (24) They're not totally wrong, but they do it wrong. (25) We have an obligation to protect our rights and challenge those who challenge us. (26) The survival of the Democratic way of life hangs in the balance.

(27) The number of books challenged has increased over the past few years. (28) Nancy Kranich, president of the American Library Association from 2000–2001, had this to say about the rise in censorship: "each time a book is challenged, restricted,

(continued on next page)

(continued from previous page)

removed, or banned, creators are less likely to express themselves. . . . (29) Teachers and librarians . . . risk their jobs and reputation when they dare to confront controversies over the public's right to read."

(30) We absolutely cannot take this freedom for granted. (31) We live in a democratic society so that we can enjoy this basic right. (32) Imagine not being able to read what you wanted to! (33) What if you couldn't read award-winning novels like the books in the *Harry Potter* series, *The Adventures of Huckleberry Finn*, *A Wrinkle in Time*, or any of your other favorites? (34) We cannot allow others to deny us the freedoms granted in the Bill of Rights.

(35) There is a reason why America stands apart from other nations and treasures its freedom of expression. (36) We cannot allow censorship of books or any other media to continue. (37) We can expect a very different America from the one we know today. (38) Technology moves us rapidly ahead, but we must remain aware of the history that gave us the ability to think and act as we do. (39) We must be free to ask questions, study, and evaluate the world around us without being restricted.

1. Choose the **best** way to write sentence 24 so that the composition maintains a consistent tone.

   They're not totally wrong, but they do it wrong.

   a. I hate them and their ideas!
   b. Censorship may be wrong, but only because it limits other people's freedoms.
   c. It's like they don't always do it right, but then they turn around and mess around with other people's lives.
   d. Their views are not necessarily wrong, but they can often have a negative impact on others' rights and freedoms.

2. Choose the correct way to write the underlined part of sentence 1.

   <u>Imagine that your at your local library</u> perusing the fiction shelves.

   a. Imagine that you're at your local library
   b. Imagine that your at you're local library
   c. Imagine that your at your local Library
   d. No change is needed.

175

3. Choose the word or phrase that **best** fits at the beginning of sentence 37.

    a. For example,
    b. However,
    c. Otherwise,
    d. Nevertheless,

4. Choose the correct way to write the underlined part of sentence 26.

    <u>The survival of the Democratic way of life hangs</u> in the balance.

    a. The survival of the democratic way of life hangs
    b. The survival of the Democratic way of life hanged
    c. The survival, of the Democratic way of life hangs
    d. No change is needed.

5. Read sentence 15, which is poorly written.

    Some of the books with controversial or disturbing subjects have been banned or challenged for their presentation of these subjects.

    Choose the **best** way to rewrite this sentence.

    a. Some of the books with controversial or disturbing subjects presented banned or challenged material.
    b. Some of the banned or challenged books were chosen for their presentation of controversial or disturbing subjects.
    c. The banned and challenged books presented controversial, disturbing subjects that had been banned or challenged.
    d. Pretty much all of the challenged books were disturbing and controversial to anyone who read them.

6. Choose the correct way to write the underlined part of sentence 5.

    Could <u>this really happen.</u>

    a. this, really happen.
    b. this really happen?
    c. this really happened.
    d. No change is needed.

7. Choose the **best** way to combine the ideas in sentences 32 and 33 into one sentence.

    Imagine not being able to read what you wanted to! What if you couldn't read award-winning novels like the books in the *Harry Potter* series, *The Adventures of Huckleberry Finn, A Wrinkle in Time*, or any of your other favorites?

    a. What if you couldn't read *The Adventures of Huckleberry Finn, A Wrinkle in Time*, or any of your other favorites, imagine that!
    b. Award-winning novels such as the *Harry Potter* series, *The Adventures of Huckleberry Finn, A Wrinkle in Time*, or any of your other favorites are imaginative.
    c. Imagine not being able to read such award-winning novels as the books in the *Harry Potter* series, *The Adventures of Huckleberry Finn, A Wrinkle in Time*, or any of your other favorites.
    d. If you couldn't read award-winning novels or your favorites, imagine what it would be like.

8. Choose the correct way to write the underlined part of sentence 10.

    To be truly effective, we must all take part <u>in the battle for the freedom to read what we chose.</u>

    a. in the battle for the freedom to reads what we chose.
    b. in the battle, for the freedom to read what we chose.
    c. in the battle for the freedom to read what we choose.
    d. No change is needed.

9. Choose the sentence that could **best** be added right after sentence 20.

    a. Television is just as healthy as reading, if not more so.
    b. If you want to read a copy of the Bill of Rights, you can visit the local library.
    c. Censors limit our freedoms many times, which makes life in America difficult.
    d. Authors sometimes intend to teach and familiarize people with unknown or uncomfortable topics.

10. Choose the correct way to write the underlined part of sentence 28.

Nancy Kranich, president of the American Library Association from 2000–2001, had this to say about the rise in censorship: "each time a book is challenged, restricted, removed, or banned, creators are less likely to express themselves. . . .

    a. "each time a book is challenged restricted, removed, or banned,
    b. "Each time a book is challenged, restricted, removed, or banned,
    c. "each time a book are challenged, restricted, removed, or banned,
    d. No change is needed.

Dena is in the seventh grade. She and the students in her English class have been asked to choose one person whom they admire and to write biographies of those persons. Dena must include reasons why the person she chose is admirable. She writes a web of ideas, researches her topic, and writes her rough draft. She needs your help editing and revising it.

Here is Dena's rough draft. Read it and then answer questions 1–10.

(1) No one could have known back in the 1970s that a hyperactive, nine-year-old nuisance would become the world's best skater. (2) When Tony Hawk first encountered a skateboard a gift from his older brother his restless ways were replaced with a serene calm. (3) Not only he go on to become the best skater; he also used his experience to help other kids who were suffering from the same frustrations to become involved in the sport.

(4) Tony Hawk was born on May 12, 1968, in San Diego, California. (5) Even at the young age of six, Tony was determined to challenge himself beyond his abilities. (6) However, he would become so frustrated if he could not meet this challenge that he would become depressed. (7) His parents grew worried about they're son's behavior and decided to have him psychologically evaluated. (8) "The psychologist said he had a 12-year-old mind in an 8-year-old body. (9) And his mind tells him he can do things his body can't do" his mother, Nancy, remembers.

(10) When Tony's brother gave him his first skateboard, a thin Bahne board, things seemed to balance out within his brain. (11) Tony found the satisfaction he had been looking for and grew calm. (12) "He started thinking about other people and became more generous," his brother recalls.

(13) Nevertheless, Tony was still challenging himself. (14) If he won a skateboarding contest but felt that he hadn't skated his best, he would grow very upset. (15) "If I don't do my best, it kills me," he said.

(16) Tony's father, Frank, encouraged him to pursue skating. (17) He drove Tony up and down the coast of California to compete in skating contests and built him a number of skate ramps. (18) Frank also founded the California Amateur Skateboard League and the national skateboard association because he was dissatisfied with the organizations that were then holding contests.

(19) Tony received a sponsorship offer from Dogtown skateboards at the age of 12 and he went pro just two years later. (20) By the age of 16, he was the best skater in the world. (21) A year later, he bought his first house; this was followed by the purchase of another when he was just 19 years old. (22) Of course, he built skate ramps on his property. (23) He married Cindy Dunbar in April 1990.

(24) Just a year later, in 1991, the popularity of skateboarding took a nosedive. (25) Tony found his income drying up and Cindy was soon supporting the family. (26) Tony

(continued on next page)

179

(continued from previous page)

sold one of his homes, as well as many of the other luxury items purchased over the years. (27) In 1992, the couple's first son, Riley, was born and Tony started Birdhouse Projects, a skateboard company with another pro skater, Per Welinder.

(28) Fortunately, skateboarding gained in popularity once again and Tony was back on top. (29) He married his current wife, Erin, in 1996. (30) Birdhouse is now one of the world's largest skateboarding companies. (31) Tony started a clothing company, which was than bought by Quiksilver in 2000. (32) He also created Tony Hawk's Pro Skater video games, which have been bestsellers since they were first released. (33) He wrote a bestselling autobiography, *Hawk—Occupation: skateboarder*, and created Tony Hawk's Gigantic Skatepark Tour for ESPN.

(34) Tony Hawk retired at the age of 31, when he stopped competitive skating. (35) He founded the Tony Hawk Foundation, a non-profit organization that helps to bring skateparks to low-income areas. (36) Tony believes that skateboarding kept it out of trouble and away from the television. (37) Tony also operates the Boom Boom HuckJam national arena tour, which features the world's best BMX bike riders, Motocross riders, and skateboarders. (38) It consistently sells out at arenas in the twenty-four cities that host it.

1.   Choose the correct way to write the underlined part of sentence 18.

     Frank also founded the California Amateur Skateboard League and the national skateboard association because he was dissatisfied with the organizations that were then holding contests.

     a.   national skateboard association because him was dissatisfied
     b.   national skateboard association because he was disatisfied
     c.   National Skateboard Association because he was dissatisfied
     d.   No change is needed.

2.   Choose the sentence that could **best** be added right after sentence 27.

     a.   Many people gathered in the early 1990s to watch Tony skate.
     b.   Tony found immediate success with his new company because the skateboarding industry was doing so well.
     c.   Riley was Tony's business partner.
     d.   However, the company did poorly at first and, two years after it was founded, Tony and Cindy divorced.

180

3. Choose the correct way to write the underlined part of sentence 7.

   His parents grew worried <u>about they're son's behavior</u> and decided to have him psychologically evaluated.

   a. about their son's behavior
   b. about they're son's behavuor
   c. about they're sons' behavior
   d. No change is needed.

4. Read sentence 2, which is poorly written.

   When Tony Hawk first encountered a skateboard a gift from his older brother his restless ways were replaced with a serene calm.

   Choose the **best** way to rewrite this sentence.

   a. When Tony Hawk first, encountered a skateboard a gift from his older brother, his restless ways were replaced with a serene calm.
   a. When Tony Hawk first encountered a skateboard a gift from his older brother, his restless ways, were replaced with a serene calm.
   a. When Tony Hawk first encountered a skateboard, a gift from his older brother his restless ways were replaced, with a serene calm.
   d. When Tony Hawk first encountered a skateboard, a gift from his older brother, his restless ways were replaced with a serene calm.

5. Choose the correct way to write the underlined part of sentence 9.

   And his mind tells him he can do things <u>his body can't do" his mother, Nancy,</u> remembers.

   a. his body can't do" his mother, Nancy
   b. his body can't do," his mother, Nancy,
   c. his body not do" his mother, Nancy,
   d. No change is needed.

6. Choose the correct way to write the underlined part of sentence 36.

   Tony believes that skateboarding kept it out of trouble and away from the television.

   a. beleives that skateboarding kept it
   b. believes that skateboarding kept him
   c. believes that skateboarding keep it
   d. No change is needed.

7. Choose the word or phrase that **best** fits at the beginning of sentence 25.

   a. Suddenly,
   b. For example,
   c. However,
   d. Regardless,

8. Choose the correct way to write the underlined part of sentence 31.

   Tony started a clothing company, which was than bought by Quiksilver in 2000.

   a. company, which was than bought by quiksilver
   b. company which was than bought by Quiksilver
   c. company, which was then bought by Quiksilver
   d. No change is needed.

9. Dena wants to add this sentence to the paragraph that begins with sentence 34.

   He wants to offer that experience to other kids who may not be as fortunate as he was to have a family so supportive of his interest.

   Where would the sentence **best** fit?

   a. right after sentence 34
   b. right after sentence 36
   c. right after sentence 37
   d. right after sentence 38

10. Choose the correct way to write the underlined part of sentence 27.

   In 1992, the couple's first son, Riley, was born and Tony started <u>Birdhouse Projects, a skateboard company with</u> another pro skater, Per Welinder.

   a. birdhouse projects, a skateboard company with
   b. Birdhouse Projects, a skateboard company, with
   c. Birdhouse Projects, a skateboard, company with
   d. No change is needed.

Caitlin's seventh-grade industrial arts class has been studying architecture and engineering. Her teacher has asked each student to write a report about a common architectural structure and describe what makes it successful. Caitlin visits the local library and researches her ideas. She has written her rough draft and needs your help editing and revising it.

Here is Caitlin's rough draft. Read it and then answer questions 1–10.

(1) Whether you're driving down the road, hiking a nature trail, or riding a train across the country, you will undoubtedly encounter one architectural marvel time and again: the bridge. (2) A bridge allows passage over some kind of obstacle, such as a river, a valley, a road, or anything that needs crossing over! (3) There are three major types of bridges, the beam, arch, and suspension bridge. (4) Most often, the type of bridge built is determined by what obstacle needs to be crossed over.

(5) Bridge types differ based on how far they stretch over a single space, or a "span." (6) A span is the distance between two bridge supports. (7) A beam bridge can span a distance of up to 200 feet. (8) An arch bridge safely spans 800–1,000 feet. (9) A suspension bridge has the furthest span—7,000 feet? (10) Whatever the type, the bridge must be able to carry a heavy load without buckling or snapping.

(11) The beam bridge is a stiff, horizontal structure that rests on two columns. (12) These columns support the weight of the bridge and any traffic on it. (13) These bridges were used a lot during the Industrial Revolution. (14) The size and height of the bridge control the distance that the beam bridge can span. (15) If a bridge designer needs the bridge to be very tall, he must add a "truss" or a supporting web, to the horizontal beam. (16) The truss adds support to the bridge and makes it able to bear more weight.

(17) The arch bridge is a semicircular structure with thick abutments. (18) The weight transfers to these abutments, making the arch bridge one of the strongest designs. (19) The arch bridge was a common design choice a long time ago. (20) Many ancient Roman arch bridges are still standing today. (21) Similar to the beam bridge, the size and height of the arch will limit the distance this bridge can reach.

(22) The suspension bridge uses cables, ropes, or chains that are strung across the obstacle being crossed. (23) The deck of the bridge is then suspended from these cables. (24) Modern suspension bridges, which can be found around the world, have two tall towers through which the cables are strung. (25) The towers, which are dug deep into the earth, support the weight of the bridge. (26) Similar to the beam bridge, many suspension bridges have a backup support system—the "truss." (27) The truss in a suspension bridge acts to keep the bridge from moving. (28) There are two types of suspension bridges: the "M" shape, featured in bridges like the golden gate bridge in San Francisco, and the "A" shape, which is less common, but becoming more popular. (29) An example of an "A" shape suspension bridge can be seen in Boston and Charleston, South Carolina.

(continued on next page)

(continued from previous page)

(30) No matter how well designed and well built a bridge is, two main forces still can destroy it. (31) Resonance and weather. (32) "Resonance" is a vibration that travels through a bridge like a wave. (33) In 1940, 40-mile-per-hour winds created resonance waves that destroyed the Tacoma Narrows Bridge. (34) The wind was hitting the bridge in just such a manner that the bridge started vibrating. (35) The resonance waves grew so large that the bridge eventually broke apart. (36) Another example of resonance would be the vibration caused when a troop of soldiers march across a bridge. (37) A large army that doesn't break the rhythm of their marching when traveling over a bridge could destroy the bridge.

(38) Weather is unpredictable and uncontrollable. (39) While new bridge designs try to compensate for the effects of rain, ice, wind, and salt, weather-related damages account for more bridge disasters than do design flaws. (40) Only preventative maintinence can be helpful.

1. Which of these is **not** a complete sentence?

   a. A bridge allows passage over some kind of obstacle, such as a river, a valley, a road, or anything that needs crossing over!
   b. A span is the distance between two bridge supports.
   c. Many ancient Roman arch bridges are still standing today.
   d. Resonance and weather.

2. Choose the correct way to write the underlined part of sentence 9.

   A suspension bridge <u>has the furthest span—7,000 feet?</u>

   a. has the farthest span—7,000 feet?
   b. has the furthest span—7,000 feet!
   c. have the furthest span—7,000 feet?
   d. No change is needed.

3. Choose the correct way to write the underlined part of sentence 28.

   There are two types of suspension bridges: the "M" shape, featured in bridges like the <u>golden gate bridge in San Francisco, and the "A" shape,</u> which is less common, but becoming more popular.

   a. Golden Gate Bridge in San Francisco, and the "A" shape,
   b. golden gate bridge in San Francisco, and the "A" shape
   c. golden gate bridge in San Francisco and the "A" shape,
   d. No change is needed.

4. Caitlin wants to change sentence 19 so that it is more specific.

    The arch bridge was a common design choice <u>a long time ago.</u>

    Choose the **best** way to rewrite the underlined part of this sentence.

    a. when people were looking for something sturdy.
    b. during the Roman, Baroque, and Renaissance periods.
    c. before there were cars and people liked them better, anyway.
    d. in places where they needed to cross over something.

5. Choose the sentence that could **best** be added right after sentence 13.

    a. A beam bridge spans distances of up to 200 feet.
    b. During the Industrial Revolution, these bridges were fairly common.
    c. Beam bridges are similar to arch and suspension bridges.
    d. Today, beam bridges can commonly be found on highway overpasses.

6. Read sentence 37, which is poorly written.

    A large army that doesn't break the rhythm of their marching when traveling over a bridge could destroy the bridge.

    Choose the **best** way to rewrite this sentence.

    a. A large army that doesn't rhythmically march over a destroyed bridge can travel over the bridge.
    b. The bridge the large army travels over makes them march rhythmically.
    c. A large army that doesn't break the rhythm of their marching when traveling over a bridge could destroy it.
    d. Rhythmic marching could destroy a bridge, so a large army doesn't break it.

7. Choose the correct way to write the underlined part of sentence 40.

Only preventative <u>maintinence can be helpful.</u>

   a. maintinence can have been helpful.
   b. maintenance can be helpful.
   c. maintinence can be helpful?
   d. No change is needed.

8. Choose the correct way to write the underlined part of sentence 15.

If a bridge designer needs the bridge to be very tall, <u>he must add a "truss" or a supporting web,</u> to the horizontal beam.

   a. he must add a "truss," or a supporting web,
   b. he must add a "truss" or, a supporting web,
   c. him must add a "truss" or a supporting web,
   d. No change is needed.

9. Read sentence 3, which is poorly written.

There are three major types of bridges, the beam, arch, and suspension bridge.

Choose the **best** way to rewrite this sentence.

   a. There are three major types of beam, arch, and suspension bridges.
   b. There are beam, arch, and suspension bridges, three major types.
   c. There are three major types: the beam, the arch, and the suspension bridge.
   d. There are three major types of bridges, the beam bridge, the arch bridge, and the suspension bridge.

10. Caitlin wants to add this sentence to the paragraph that begins with sentence 17.

Arches made of stone, in fact, don't even need any mortar to hold the stones together.

Where would the sentence **best** fit?

   a. right after sentence 17
   b. right after sentence 18
   c. right after sentence 20
   d. right after sentence 21

187

Jan's seventh-grade history class has been studying how technology unites foreign countries. His teacher has asked that each student write about a topic of his or her choosing that would illustrate this idea. Jan chooses his topic and writes his rough draft. He needs your help editing and revising it.

Here is Jan's rough draft. Read it and then answer questions 1–10.

(1) The first air race was held in Rheims, France, in August 1909, just six years after the Wright brothers's first flight. (2) Spectators, some of whom had never seen an airplane before, gathered to watch the pilots compete for prizes. (3) An American, Glenn H. Curtiss, won the two biggest prizes: the James Gordon Bennett Trophy for the fastest two laps and the *Prix de la Vitesse* for the fastest three laps. (4) Air racing was born.

(5) The first United States air race was held in Los Angeles less than a year later. (6) Curtiss set a record of 55 miles per hour for a plane with one passenger. (7) In October 1910, the second international meet was held in Elmont, New York. (8) The Bennett Trophy race attracted dozens of planes and pilots from Europe and the United States. (9) During World War I, Bennett Trophy racing was suspended. (10) Many races were postponed until the war ended. (11) In 1920, the French won their third consecutive Bennett Trophy, thus retiring the trophy and ending this competition.

(12) Other trophies were offered to the best air race pilots. (13) The Michelin Cup was awarded for the longest flight between sunrise and sundown on a single day. (14) Orville Wright won the first competition for this trophy in 1908. (15) The *London Daily Mail* prize was awarded for the first flight over the English channel. (16) In 1909, Louis Bleriot of France won it. (17) After World War I, in 1919, two British military pilots won the £10,000 prize for flying nonstop between England and America. (18) The Jacques Schneider Trophy was initiated in 1913, and was for seaplane races over open water. (19) It, too, was suspended during World War I, but resumed following the war. (20) The $25,000 prize offered, in 1919, by a New York hotel owner for a nonstop flight between New York and France would ultimately led to the famous Charles Lindbergh flight. (21) Lindbergh claimed this prize in 1927.

(22) The Pulitzer Trophy for international air races held in America was announced in 1919. (23) The first race was held in 1920 on Long Island. (24) Charles Moseley took home the trophy for averaging 156.5 miles per hour over a closed-circuit course. (25) As many as 25,000 spectators gathered to watch. (26) In 1921, a national air meet was established. (27) It later became known as the National Air Races.

(28) The John L. Mitchell Trophy meets, begun in 1924, were the first air races to set planes against other planes on a closed-circuit course. (29) These races were very popular among spectators. (30) By 1929, there were 27 similar closed-circuit events at the National Air Races. (31) One of these events was the Women's Air Derby, which began on August 13th in California and ended on August 20th in Cleveland. (32) Among the twenty competiters was Amelia Earhart. (33) This event led to the establishment of

(continued on next page)

(continued from previous page)

the All-Woman Transcontinental Air Race, or what was called the "Powder Puff Derby," after World War II.

(34) The Great Depression took its toll on air racing and attendance numbers declined during the 1930s. (35) Nevertheless, the National Air Races continued until 1939. (36) With the importance of airplanes in World War II the popularity of air races grew once again. (37) The National Air Races started up in 1946 in Cleveland. (38) This time, they were sponsored by the War Department. (39) In 1949, an accident occurred when a prop plane crashed into a house. (40) The pilot and a mother and her child were all killed. (41) The National Air Races became stunted for a time.

(42) But air racing would not die. (43) The National Air Show began in 1951 and involved primarily military planes. (44) The Defense Department ruled in 1957 that military aircraft could no longer take part in the contest so the National Air Show was discontinued. (45) Some people's passion for racing kept the sport alive. (46) They formed what would become the National Air-Racing Group; this existed until 1964 when Reno revived the National Air Races as part of the centennial celebration of Nevada's statehood. (47) Drawing hundreds of thousands of fans from around the world, the competition still goes on today.

1. Choose the correct way to write the underlined part of sentence 36.

With the importance of airplanes <u>in World War II the popularity of air races</u> grew once again.

   a. in World War II the popularity of Air Races
   b. in World War II the popularity of, air races
   c. in World War II, the popularity of air races
   d. No change is needed.

2. Choose the sentence that could **best** be added right after sentence 11.

   a. There may or may not have been Swedish pilots in this race.
   b. The Bennett Trophy had already been won by an American.
   c. Although the French had won many trophies, the fact that they had never won the Bennett Trophy truly aggravated them.
   d. Frenchman Jules Vedrines, who won the trophy in 1912, was the first pilot to average more than 100 miles per hour.

3. Choose the correct way to write the underlined part of sentence 20.

The $25,000 prize offered, in 1919, by a New York hotel owner for a nonstop flight between New York and France would <u>ultimately led to the famous Charles Lindbergh flight.</u>

    a. ultimately led to the famous charles lindbergh flight.
    b. ultimately lead to the famous Charles Lindbergh flight.
    c. ultimatly led to the famous Charles Lindbergh flight.
    d. No change is needed.

4. Read sentence 44, which is poorly written.

The Defense Department ruled in 1957 that military aircraft could no longer take part in the contest so the National Air Show was discontinued.

Choose the **best** way to rewrite this sentence.

    a. In 1957, when the Defense Department ruled that military aircraft could no longer take part in the contest, the National Air Show was discontinued.
    b. The National Air Show ruled that military aircraft could no longer take part in the contest in 1957, so the Defense Department was discontinued.
    c. The National Department, in 1957, ruled that the Defense Air Show could no longer include military aircraft and, thus, it should be discontinued.
    d. The Defense Department could no longer allow military aircraft in the contest, so the National Air Show was discontinued, in 1957.

5. Choose the correct way to write the underlined part of sentence 15.

The *London Daily Mail* prize was awarded for <u>the first flight over the English channel.</u>

    a. the first flight, over the English channel.
    b. the first flight over the English Channel.
    c. the first flight over the English channel?
    d. No change is needed.

6. Jan wants to add this sentence to the paragraph that begins with sentence 42.

   Many were former fighter pilots who had bought war surplus planes, civilians who had built their own small planes, or antique aircraft enthusiasts who owned old biplanes.

   Where would the sentence **best** fit?

   a. right after sentence 43
   b. right after sentence 45
   c. right after sentence 46
   d. right after sentence 47

7. Choose the correct way to write the underlined part of sentence 1.

   The first air race was held in Rheims, France, in August 1909, <u>just six years after the Wright brothers's first flight.</u>

   a. just six years after the Wright brothers' first flight.
   b. just six years, after the Wright brothers's first flight.
   c. just six years after the Wright brothers's first flight?
   d. No change is needed.

8. Choose the word or phrase that **best** fits at the beginning of sentence 10.

   a. However,
   b. Nevertheless,
   c. For instance,
   d. In fact,

9. Choose the correct way to write the underlined part of sentence 32.

   <u>Among the twenty competiters</u> was Amelia Earhart.

   a. Among the twentey competiters
   b. Amoung the twenty competiters
   c. Among the twenty competitors
   d. No change is needed.

10. Read sentence 18, which is poorly written.

   The Jacques Schneider Trophy was initiated in 1913, and was for seaplane races over open water.

   Choose the **best** way to rewrite this sentence.

   a. The Jacques Schneider Trophy, initiated in 1913, was for seaplane races over open water.
   b. The Jacques Schneider Trophy was for seaplane races over open water, initiated in 1913.
   c. In 1913, the Jacques Schneider Trophy was for seaplane races initiated over open water.
   d. The seaplane races over open water, in 1913, were awarded the Jacques Schneider Trophy.

Krystal's seventh-grade social studies class has recently been looking at symbols that characterize American style and traditions. Her teacher asks the students to write reports describing objects of some kind that are commonly tied to United States culture. Krystal has spent some time at the local library and written her report. She needs your help editing and revising it.

Here is Krystal's rough draft. Read it and then answer questions 1–10.

(1) Converse™ sneakers are a symbol of American culture and tradition. (2) They have been used in sports and for casaul wear for almost a century. (3) The company offers several footwear and clothing for sports performance, sports classics, and sports lifestyle for men, women, and children.

(4) Converse was established by Marquis M. Converse in 1908. (5) The company calls itself "America's Original Sports Company." (6) Their shoes have been tied to such sports as basketball, tennis turf, and track. (7) The Converse All Star®, introduced in 1917, was the world's first performance basketball shoe.

(8) Basketball, which derived from the Converse All Star, was revolutionized by the Chuck Taylor® All Star. (9) It was commonly worn among basketball players, around the world for almost fifty years. (10) "Chucks," Cons," or "Connies," as they have been called, were first introduced in 1923. (11) To date, more than 750 million pairs have been sold in 144 countries.

(12) For much of the twentieth century, Converse shoes were dominant on the basketball court. (13) Legends such as Julius Erving ("Dr. J"), an amazing talent from the 1970s, made the Pro Leather, Pro Star, and Weapon™ basketball shoes popular. (14) The new designs of the shoes offered an opportunity to gain speed and agility, while exhibited creativity and self-expression. (15) Converse still provides basketball footwear today.

(16) Converse shoes can be found far off the basketball court, too. (17) They have become a common trend among Americas youth, who are often drawn to their original, unique look and creative designs. (18) The Jack Purcell® shoe, named for a famous badminton champion, came on the scene in 1935 with the well-known Smile™ on the front. (19) The Converse One Star® is popular in the surf and skate community.

(20) Converse shoes have always characterized creativity and self-expression. (21) Many Americans value these traits. (22) People can often gain an impression of someone just by seeing how him or her is dressed. (23) Converse offers footwear and clothing for unique, creative people who want to make a bold statement. (24) What better expression of United States culture is there?

1. Choose the correct way to write the underlined part of sentence 6.

   Their shoes have been tied to such <u>sports as basketball, tennis turf, and track.</u>

   a. sports as Basketball, Tennis Turf, and Track.
   b. sports, as basketball, tennis turf, and track.
   c. sports as basketball, tennis, turf, and track.
   d. No change is needed.

2. Choose the correct way to write the underlined part of sentence 9.

   It was commonly worn among <u>basketball players, around the world</u> for almost fifty years.

   a. Basketball Players, around the world
   b. basketball players around the world
   c. basketball players, around the World
   d. No change is needed.

3. Choose the correct way to write the underlined part of sentence 22.

   People can often gain an impression of someone just <u>by seeing how him or her is dressed.</u>

   a. by seeing how, him or her is dressed.
   b. by seeing how he or she is dressed.
   c. by seeing how him or her is dress.
   d. No change is needed.

4. Choose the correct way to write the underlined part of sentence 10.

   <u>"Chucks," Cons," or "Connies,"</u> as they have been called, were first introduced in 1923.

   a. "Chucks" Cons" or "Connies"
   b. "Chucks, Cons, or Connies,"
   c. "Chucks," "Cons," or "Connies,"
   d. No change is needed.

5. Read sentence 3, which is poorly written.

    The company offers several footwear and clothing for sports performance, sports classics, and sports lifestyle for men, women, and children.

    Choose the **best** way to rewrite this sentence.

    a. The company offers collections of men's, women's, and children's footwear and clothing for sports performance, classics, and lifestyle.
    b. Men, women, and children can get several kinds of footwear and clothing from the company for sports performance and sports lifestyle.
    c. Several of footwears and clothings from the company can be had for men, women, and children for sports performance, sports classics, and sports lifestyle.
    d. Sports performance, sports classics, and sports lifestyle are offered by the company. They are available for men and women.

6. Krystal wants to add this sentence to the paragraph that begins with sentence 16.

    These shoes were popular in early Hollywood and among boarding-school "bad boys."

    Where would the sentence **best** fit?

    a. right after sentence 16
    b. right after sentence 17
    c. right after sentence 18
    d. right after sentence 19

7. Choose the correct way to write the underlined part of sentence 2.

    They have been used <u>in sports and for casaul wear</u> for almost a century.

    a. in sports and for casual wear
    b. in sports, and for casaul wear
    c. in sports' and for casaul wear
    d. No change is needed.

8. Choose the correct way to write the underlined part of sentence 17.

   They have become <u>a common trend among Americas youth,</u> who are often drawn to their original, unique look and creative designs.

   a. a common trend among Americas Youth,
   b. a common trend, among Americas youth,
   c. a common trend among America's youth,
   d. No change is needed.

9. Choose the correct way to write the underlined part of sentence 14.

   The new designs of the shoes offered an opportunity to gain speed and agility, <u>while exhibited creativity and self-expression.</u>

   a. while exhibited creativety and self-expression.
   b. while exhibited creativity, and self-expression.
   c. while exhibiting creativity and self-expression.
   d. No change is needed.

10. Read sentence 8, which is poorly written.

   Basketball, which derived from the Converse All Star, was revolutionized by the Chuck Taylor® All Star.

   Choose the **best** way to rewrite this sentence.

   a. The Chuck Taylor® All Star, which derived from the Converse All Star, was revolutionized by basketball.
   b. The Chuck Taylor® All Star was revolutionized by basketball, which derived from the Converse All Star.
   c. The Converse All Star revolutionized basketball, and derived from the Chuck Taylor® All Star.
   d. The Chuck Taylor® All Star, which derived from the Converse All Star, revolutionized basketball.

Grover's assignment for his seventh-grade science class is to choose a toy that he remembers playing with when he was younger and write a report about how scientific principles relate to it. Grover selects his favorite childhood toy, researches how it works, and writes a rough draft. He needs your help editing and revising it.

Here is Grover's rough draft. Read it and then answer questions 1–10.

(1) In 1974, four engineers at the pilot pen corporation invented one of the most popular drawing toys. (2) Today, more than 40 million have sold. (3) The invention was the Magna Doodle™. (4) The Magna Doodle is not only a fun, creative toy; it is also a scientific study of magnitizm.

(5) The basic Magna Doodle is made up of several parts: a white, plastic screen on which to draw; a pen with a magnet at the tip that is attached by a string; a magnet that works to erase the screen; and the case in which the mechanism is contained. (6) These parts all work together to create a "dustless chalkboard" that has been used by underwater divers, coaches, and teachers, as well as on road trips and in the home. (7) There is less mess and less waste in using the Magna Doodle instead of paper or traditional chalkboards.

(8) The white, plastic screen is technically called a "magnetophoretic display panel. (9) It is made up of three layers. (10) The front and back are pieces of transparent or semi-transparent plastic. (11) The middle is a honeycombed or hexagonal plastic web. (12) Each cell of the web is filled with a thick liquid substance that contains many tiny magnetic particles. (13) The pen and eraser pull the dark, small, fine particles around to create (or erase) drawings and writing.

(14) The magnetic pen has a small magnet at the tip, which is strong enough to pull the particles through the liquid. (15) The liquid is thick. (16) The magnetic particles are prevented from sinking because of this, so what is drawn can be seen over time. (17) White dye is mixed into the liquid to provide a contrast between the particles and the liquid. (18) This is why the drawing is so easy to see.

(19) The eraser is actually a bar magnet that slides back and forth to pull the magnetic particles, from the front of the magnetophoretic display to the back. (20) It seem to magically disappear! (21) They are nearly invisible behind the thick liquid. (22) They are also being held to the back of the display until the magnetic pen is used pulling them to the front.

(23) It is amazing that a child's toy could be so intricate. (24) There are so many things going on to make my drawings appear and reappear. (25) Science aside, however, the Magna Doodle is just a really fun toy to play with!

1. Choose the correct way to write the underlined part of sentence 19.

    The eraser is actually a bar magnet that slides <u>back and forth to pull the magnetic particles, from the front</u> of the magnetophoretic display to the back.

    a. back and forth to pulled the magnetic particles, from the front
    b. back and forth to pull, the magnetic particles, from the front
    c. back and forth to pull the magnetic particles from the front
    d. No change is needed.

2. Choose the correct way to write the underlined part of sentence 1.

    In 1974, <u>four engineers at the pilot pen corporation</u> invented one of the most popular drawing toys.

    a. for engineers at the pilot pen corporation
    b. four engineers at the Pilot Pen Corporation
    c. four engineers, at the pilot pen corporation
    d. No change is needed.

3. Choose the correct way to write the underlined part of sentence 13.

    The pen and eraser pull <u>the dark, small, fine particles around to create</u> (or erase) drawings and writing.

    a. the dark, small, fine particles around to create,
    b. the dark, small fine particles around to create
    c. the dark, small, fine particles around to creates
    d. No change is needed.

4. Choose the **best** way to combine the ideas in sentences 15 and 16 into one sentence.

The liquid is thick. The magnetic particles are prevented from sinking because of this, so what is drawn can be seen over time.

   a.   The thickness of the liquid prevents the magnetic particles from sinking, so that what is drawn can be seen over time.
   b.   What is drawn can be seen over time, which prevents the magnetic particles from sinking in the thick liquid.
   c.   Over time, the thick liquid prevents the magnetic particles from sinking, so what is drawn can be seen over time.
   d.   The magnetic particles, from sinking in the thick liquid, so what can be seen over time is drawn.

5. Choose the correct way to write the underlined part of sentence 4.

The Magna Doodle is not only a fun, creative toy; it <u>is also a scientific study of magnitizm.</u>

   a.   was also a scientific study of magnitizm.
   b.   is also a scientific study of magnetism.
   c.   is also a scientific, study of magnitizm.
   d.   No change is needed.

6. Choose the correct way to write the underlined part of sentence 20.

<u>It seem to</u> magically disappear!

   a.   It seem too
   b.   Its seem to
   c.   It seems to
   d.   No change is needed.

7. Choose the word or phrase that **best** fits at the beginning of sentence 21.

   a.   However,
   b.   For example,
   c.   In fact,
   d.   Moreover,

8. Read sentence 7, which is poorly written.

   There is less mess and less waste in using the Magna Doodle instead of paper or traditional chalkboards.

   Choose the **best** way to rewrite this sentence.

   a. Traditional chalkboards and paper create less mess and less waste than the Magna Doodle.
   b. Less mess and less waste are created by using Magna Doodle instead of paper or traditional chalkboards, both of which create a big mess and a lot of waste.
   c. The Magna Doodle uses paper and traditional chalkboards to make less mess and less waste.
   d. Using the Magna Doodle instead of paper or traditional chalkboards creates less mess and less waste.

9. Choose the correct way to write the underlined part of sentence 22.

   They are also being held to the back of the display until the magnetic pen is <u>used pulling them to the front.</u>

   a. used to pull them to the front.
   b. used pulling them, to the front.
   c. used pulling them to the front?
   d. No change is needed.

10. Choose the correct way to write the underlined part of sentence 8.

   The white, plastic screen is technically <u>called a "magnetophoretic display panel.</u>

   a. called a, "magnetophoretic display panel.
   b. called a "Magnetophoretic display panel.
   c. called a "magnetophoretic display panel."
   d. No change is needed.

Karina's seventh-grade English teacher selects one student every three weeks to write a report on a poet of his or her choosing. It is Karina's turn. Since she wants to be a poet herself, Karina enthusiastically begins her research. She has written her rough draft, but needs your help editing and revising it.

Here is Karina's rough draft. Read it and then answer questions 1–10.

(1) Margaret Atwood is among the world's most prolific female writers of the past one hundred years. (2) Margaret was born on November 18, 1939, in Ottawa Canada. (3) This was nearly three months before the advent of World War II. (4) As early as May 1940, her father, who was doing research as a forest entomologist, took her to the forest of northwestern Quebec. (5) Her parents were unconventional for the time. (6) They avoided civilization and did not strive to become the everyday 1940s household. (7) As a result, Margaret spent much of her young life in the woods and by herself. (8) She learned to read early on and spent much of her time reading anything she could find.

(9) Margaret created her first poetry book at the age of five. (10) It held all the poems she could remember. (11) It had nursery rhymes and some of her own first original works at the end. (12) She would not write again for another eleven years. (13) At the age of sixteen, the year being 1956, Margaret was in her fourth year of high school in Toronto. (14) She crossed the football field on her way home from school when, as she described it, "a large invisible thumb descended from the sky and pressed down on the top of my head. (15) A poem formed. (16) It was quite a gloomy poem: the poems of the young usually are. (17) It was a gift, this poem, . . . both exciting and sinister at the same time."

(18) Margaret said that her ignorance of any poetry written after the year 1900 meant that she had virtually no knowledge of free verse. (19) Her first "real" poem rhymed and was filled with dark themes, such as those she had read in Lord Byron or Edgar Allan Poe's works. (20) Nevertheless, she contends that on that day in 1956, she officially became a poet. (21) Her former English teacher, who were studying the author's life, told some documentary filmmakers that Margaret had shown no particular promise in her class. (22) No doubt she was surprised to find that Margaret would later become one of the most famous female poets of all time.

(23) Of course, Margaret does admit that she, as a poet, remained ignorant for a good many years after that day as well. (24) While no one told her outright that she couldn't be a poet, most people in 1950s Canada considered an occupation as a writer to be absurd. (25) When her twelfth-grade English teacher, Miss Bessie Billings, finally read her poetry, Margaret received this response: "I can't understand a word of this, dear, so it must be good." (26) This brief word of encouragement was more then she had ever received.

(27) After working in journalism and studying English literature (where she finally realized that not all poetry had to rhyme), Margaret began publishing in small magazines and writing reviews. (28) She put together a collection of poems for publication. (29) But was rejected time and time again. (30) While she knew that her poetry was

(continued on next page)

(continued from previous page)

getting better, she also knew she could not make a living at it unless she took a more active role. (31) She decided to self-publish a collection of her work. (32) Today, those small booklets are worth over $1,800 each.

(33) Several years went by and Margaret began teaching grammar to engineering students in british columbia. (34) She describes this time vividly: "I taught in the daytime, ate canned food, [and] did not wash my dishes until all of them were dirty." (35) In that year, she also completed her first published book of poems, *The Circle Game*, as well as her first published novel. (36) The poetry book won the coveted Governor General's Award.

(37) She continues to write today, balancing writing novels and poetry, so that she won't go "slowly down a long dark tunnel with no exit." (38) Margaret Atwood always finds that when she writes poetry, it still is as surprising and mysterious as when that hand descended in 1956.

1. Read sentence 21, which is poorly written.

   Her former English teacher, who were studying the author's life, told some documentary filmmakers that Margaret had shown no particular promise in her class.

   Choose the **best** way to rewrite this sentence.

   a. Her former English teacher, who were studying the author's life, told some documentary filmmakers that the teacher had shown no particular promise in Margaret's class.
   b. Margaret had shown no particular promise in the class of her former English teacher, who were studying the author's life, she told some documentary filmmakers.
   c. Her former English teacher told some documentary filmmakers, who were studying the author's life, that Margaret had shown no particular promise in her class.
   d. Some documentary filmmakers told Margaret that she had shown no particular promise in her former English teacher's class.

2. Choose the correct way to write the underlined part of sentence 26.

   This brief word of encouragement was more <u>then she had ever received.</u>

   a. than she had ever received.
   b. then she had ever recieved.
   c. then her had ever received.
   d. No change is needed.

202

3. Karina wants to add this sentence to the paragraph that begins with sentence 27.

   She printed 250 copies and sold them for 50 cents each.

   Where would the sentence **best** fit?

   a. right after sentence 27
   b. right after sentence 28
   c. right after sentence 30
   d. right after sentence 31

4. Choose the correct way to write the underlined part of sentence 2.

   Margaret was born <u>on November 18, 1939, in Ottawa Canada.</u>

   a. on November 18 1939, in Ottawa Canada.
   b. on November 18, 1939, in Ottawa, Canada.
   c. on November 18, 1939, in Ottawa Canada!
   d. No change is needed.

5. Choose the **best** way to combine the ideas in sentences 10 and 11 into one sentence.

   It held all the poems she could remember. It had nursery rhymes and some of her own first original works at the end.

   a. It had some of her own first original works and some nursery rhymes at the end.
   b. It held nursery rhymes and some of her own first original works, all the ones she could remember, anyway.
   c. It had all the poems she could remember and some of her own at the end.
   d. It held a collection of all the poems she could remember, such as nursery rhymes, with some of her own first original works at the end.

6. Choose the correct way to write the underlined part of sentence 33.

Several years went by and Margaret began teaching <u>grammar to engineering students in british columbia.</u>

   a. grammer to engineering students in british columbia.
   b. grammar to engineering students, in british columbia.
   c. grammar to engineering students in British Columbia.
   d. No change is needed.

7. Which of these is **not** a complete sentence?

   a. No doubt she was surprised to find that Margaret would later become one of the most famous female poets of all time.
   b. When her twelfth-grade English teacher, Miss Bessie Billings, finally read her poetry, Margaret received this response: "I can't understand a word of this, dear, so it must be good."
   c. But was rejected time and time again.
   d. The poetry book won the coveted Governor General's Award.

8. Choose the correct way to write the underlined part of sentence 14.

<u>She crossed the football field on her way home</u> from school when, as she described it, "a large invisible thumb descended from the sky and pressed down on the top of my head.

   a. She was crossing the football field on her way home
   b. She crossed the football field, on her way home
   c. She crossed the Football field on her way home
   d. No change is needed.

9.   Read sentence 8, which is poorly written.

She learned to read early on and spent much of her time reading anything she could find.

Choose the **best** way to rewrite this sentence.

a.   She learned how to read early on, so she read a lot.
b.   She learned how to read early on and spent much of her time buried in any book she could find.
c.   She learned how to read early on and spent much of her time reading, almost as much time as she spent learning how to read.
d.   She learned how to read early on, so she read anything she could find.

10. Read sentence 38, which is poorly written.

Margaret Atwood always finds that when she writes poetry, it still is as surprising and mysterious as when that hand descended in 1956.

Choose the **best** way to rewrite this sentence.

a.   She always is still surprising and mysterious as when that hand descended in 1956 whenever she writes poetry.
b.   Writing poetry still surprises and mystifies Margaret Atwood like she writes it by hand.
c.   Margaret Atwood finds that writing poetry is still as surprising and mysterious as when that hand descended upon her in 1956.
d.   She always is surprised and mystified by writing poetry, just like when that hand descended in 1956 and surprised her.

Miles lives in Chicago, Illinois. Miles's seventh-grade class has recently taken a trip to the brand-new Millennium Park in Chicago. His history teacher asks each student to write a letter to a friend who hasn't visited the park, describing the features of the park and persuading that person to plan a trip. Miles makes a brief outline to map out his ideas and writes his rough draft. He needs your help editing and revising it.

Here is Miles's rough draft. Read it and then answer questions 1–10.

(1) Dear Pedro,

(2) I just got back from visiting the Millennium Park in Chicago and I had to write to tell you about it. (3) Pedro, it is incredible! (4) You can see some incredible examples of modern art there. (5) I think it's going to draw tourists to the city for many, many years.

(6) The park opened on July 16th and drew tens of thousands of people. (7) Most of these visitors probably remember what was there before: a railroad yard and a parking lot. (8) Now, the 24-acre park presents a beautiful view. (9) As well as more money for the city. (10) It has a stainless-steel pavilion for concerts and a pedestrian bridge. (11) Frank Gehry designed them. (12) The park also has a unique, reflective, teardrop-shaped sculpture by Anish Kapoor. (13) People are already calling it the "Bean"! (14) The real name of the sculpture is "Cloud Gate." (15) It is sixty-six feet long and thirty-three feet high. (16) People were standing in front of it, waving, and taking pictures of themselves. (17) It was to funny.

(18) The park also has Crown Fountain by Jaume Plensa. (19) The little kids at the park really liked this the best. (20) It is a gigantic fountain with water cascading off two 50-foot video screen towers. (21) The screens shows pictures of Chicago and its residents. (22) About every five minutes or so, a gigantic face would shoot a stream of water out of its mouth. (23) The little kids would go crazy!

(24) There is also a public theater, a bicycle station, a promenade, and an ice rink. (25) One of the best features of the park is Frank Gehry's Pritzker Pavilion, which offers the most amazing acoustics in the city. (26) Although it is close to heavy traffic areas like Michigan avenue and Columbus drive, the sound in the pavilion cannot be muted. (27) For the most part, the orchestra, chorus, and solo singers could be heard clearly from any point in the park. (28) Almost 100 speakers hang 30 feet above the audience. (29) Overhead is a crisscross metal trellis of stainless steel. (30) The sound produced was awe-inspiring.

(31) Its interesting that the park that was supposed to be launched at the dawn of the millennium didn't actually open until 2004. (32) It was also supposed to cost the city about $150 million dollars, but by the time it was finished, it was up to $475 million dollars. (33) Some residents have complained that the amount of money spent on building the park has hurt other local projects. (34) Mayor Richard Daley doesn't seem

(continued on next page)

(continued from previous page)

to mind, though, as he sees Millennium Park as a centerpiece of his grand vision for beautifying the city.

(35) When you come back to Chicago, I'd love to take you to Millennium Park. (36) I plan on going many, many more times to enjoy all the new sights and sounds. (37) I hope to hear from you soon!

(38) Your Friend,

(39) Miles

1. Choose the correct way to write the underlined part of sentence 17.

It was <u>to funny.</u>

   a. too funny.
   b. to funny?
   c. to funnier.
   d. No change is needed.

2. Choose the sentence that could **best** be added right after sentence 27.

   a. The pavilion was designed to feel like an enclosed space for the 4,000 people sitting in fixed seats and the 7,000 people sitting in the lawn area.
   b. The mayor was very excited about the new features of the park.
   c. Children who were playing in the fountain seemed to like the bicycle station and the ice rink, too.
   d. Whenever I come to the park, I get the feeling that I'm standing in a parking lot.

3. Choose the correct way to write the underlined part of sentence 21.

<u>The screens shows pictures of Chicago</u> and its residents.

   a. The screen's shows pictures of Chicago
   b. The screens shows pictures of chicago
   c. The screens show pictures of Chicago
   d. No change is needed.

4. Choose the correct way to write line 38, the closing of the letter.

Your Friend,

  a. You're Friend,
  b. Your friend,
  c. Your Friend
  d. No change is needed.

5. The paragraph that begins with sentence 2 is poorly written. Choose the **best** way to rewrite sentence 4 so that the paragraph does not repeat ideas.

You can see some incredible examples of modern art there.

  a. Modern art is there and you can see it if you go there.
  b. If you go there, you can see incredible examples of modern art.
  c. There, you can see incredible examples of modern art.
  d. You can see some remarkable examples of modern art there.

6. Miles wants to add this sentence to the paragraph that begins with sentence 31.

Almost half of that money was raised by private donations from wealthy Chicago families, and the rest came from the city and corporations.

Where would the sentence **best** fit?

  a. right after sentence 31
  b. right after sentence 32
  c. right after sentence 33
  d. right after sentence 34

7. Choose the correct way to write the underlined part of sentence 26.

Although it is close to heavy <u>traffic areas like Michigan avenue and Columbus drive,</u> the sound in the pavilion cannot be muted.

  a. traffic areas like Michigan avenue and Columbus drive
  b. traffic area like Michigan avenue and Columbus drive,
  c. traffic areas like Michigan Avenue and Columbus Drive,
  d. No change is needed.

8. Which of these is **not** a complete sentence?

    a. As well as more money for the city.
    b. The little kids would go crazy!
    c. Almost 100 speakers hang 30 feet above the audience.
    d. I hope to hear from you soon!

9. Choose the correct way to write the underlined part of sentence 31.

    <u>Its interesting that the park that</u> was supposed to be launched at the dawn of the millennium didn't actually open until 2004.

    a. Its interested that the park that
    b. It's interesting that the park that
    c. Its interesting, that the park that
    d. No change is needed.

10. Read sentence 32, which is poorly written.

    It was also supposed to cost the city about $150 million dollars, but by the time it was finished, it was up to $475 million dollars.

    Choose the **best** way to rewrite this sentence.

    a. While the supposed cost of the project was about $150 million, the price had risen to $475 million by the time it was finished.
    b. It did cost $150 million dollars, but then it cost an additional $475, to build the park.
    c. The cost of the park was supposed to be about $150 million dollars, but the price went up to $475 million dollars eventually by the time it was finished.
    d. The park cost of $150 million dollars skyrocketed to $475 million dollars when it was finally finished.

Alexis's seventh-grade environmental science teacher gave the class the following writing prompt and asked them to write reports in response to it: *Imagine it is fifty years into the future. Think about how you might perceive the environmental problems in existence today. Write a letter to someone in the present time, telling him or her about what technology he or she could be using today to help to improve air quality in New York City.* Alexis has devised a web of ideas and has written her rough draft. She needs your help editing and revising it.

Here is Alexis's rough draft. Read it and then answer questions 1–10.

(1) Dear Mr. Sellers,

(2) If you're like most people, you probably drive a gas-powered car. (3) You may be aware of the toxins you are releasing into the environment, as well as the collective harm caused by all of those cars, trucks, vans, and SUVs on the roadways. (4) There are steps you could take to improve the air quality around you. (5) Have you ever thought about traveling on air?

(6) Gasoline is expensive, and when you consider all of the harm it does to the environment, you should be seeking alternatives. (7) Furthermore, gasoline will at some point disappear altogether, so people must have an alternative means of getting around. (8) One not so dependent upon this non-renewable resource. (9) In your lifetime, hybrid cars have become an option. (10) Alternative engines power these vehicles. (11) These include electric and fuel-cell-powered types of engines.

(12) Consider the e.Volution car, an air-powered vehicle introduced by Zero Pollution Motors in Brignoles France. (13) The exhaust from the e.Volution's engine will not contain pollutants. (14) The compressed air that fuels the car lasts for up to 124 miles and reaches speeds as high as 60 miles per hour. (15) Instead of refueling at the gas pump, however, you can just fill up at the most near air pump! (16) Furthermore, you would only have to change the oil every 31,000 miles, instead of every 3,000 like most of your modern-day vehicles.

(17) Not long after the news broke about this revolutionary new technology, the Mexican government signed a deal to buy 40,000 e.Volutions to use as taxis. (18) (Mexico City is extremely polluted.) (19) Due to the fact that the e.Volution car runs on air, the company claimed that it caused low levels of pollution or no pollution at all. (20) However, some critics say that the car does contribute to pollution because the electricity used to help power the car comes from fossil fuels. (21) Regardless, these cars would be better for the environment.

(22) Another air-powered car, the LN2000, which is being developed at the University of Wisconsin, is based upon the concept of the steam engine. (23) The scientists involved in these experiments decided to use nitrogen because it is so abundant because

(continued on next page)

210

(continued from previous page)

it makes up about 78 percent of the Earth's atmosphere. (24) The liquid nitrogen used to power this car is stored at −320 degrees Fahrenheit. (25) The nitrogen is heated to a boil and then turns to gas just like boiling water turns into steam.

(26) The LN2000 gives off very little pollution because releasing nitrogen back into the atmosphere is relatively harmless. (27) The LN2000 does produce the same type of pollution as the e.Volution; electricity is used to power the car and fossil fuels are being used to create that electricity.

(28) Right now, it may be difficult for you to envision your weekly commute without the inevitable—and costly—visit to the gas pumps. (29) However, in less time then you can imagine, gasoline-powered vehicles will be things of the past. (30) The influx of SUVs and the abundance of drivers on the roads are detrimental to the environment. (31) It is time to consider a more realistic alternative.

(32) Your Friend from the Future,

(33) Alexis

1. Choose the correct way to write the underlined part of sentence 12.

   Consider the e.Volution car, an air-powered vehicle <u>introduced by Zero Pollution Motors in Brignoles France.</u>

   a. introduced by Zero Pollution Motors in Brignoles, France.
   b. introduced, by Zero Pollution Motors in Brignoles France.
   c. introduced by zero pollution motors in Brignoles France.
   d. No change is needed.

2. Choose the word or phrase that **best** fits at the beginning of sentence 27.

   a. For example,
   b. Moreover,
   c. As a result,
   d. Nonetheless,

3. Choose the correct way to write the underlined part of sentence 15.

    Instead of refueling at the gas pump, however, you can just <u>fill up at the most near air pump!</u>

    a. fill up at, the most near air pump!
    b. fill up at the nearest air pump!
    c. fill up at the most near air pump.
    d. No change is needed.

4. Read sentence 20, which is poorly written.

    However, some critics say that the car does contribute to pollution because the electricity used to help power the car comes from fossil fuels.

    Choose the **best** way to rewrite this sentence.

    a. However, some critics say that's wrong. They say that the car does contribute to pollution. The electricity used to help power the car comes from fossil fuels.
    b. However, some critics disagree, stating that the electricity used to help power the car comes from fossil fuels.
    c. Because the electricity used to help power the car comes from fossil fuels, however, the car does contribute to pollution.
    d. If you want to listen to what the critics say, then you'll hear that this car and its electricity contribute to pollution.

5. Choose the correct way to write line 32, the closing of the letter.

    Your Friend from the Future,

    a. Your Freind from the Future,
    b. Your Friend From The Future,
    c. Your friend from the future,
    d. No change is needed.

6. Read sentence 23, which is poorly written.

    The scientists involved in these experiments decided to use nitrogen because it is so abundant because it makes up about 78 percent of the Earth's atmosphere.

    Choose the **best** way to rewrite this sentence.

    a. The scientists involved in these experiments decided to use the abundant element nitrogen, which makes up about 78 percent of the Earth's atmosphere.
    b. The Earth's atmosphere, which makes up about 78 percent of all nitrogen, was used by scientists involved in these experiments.
    c. Nitrogen, the abundant element used by scientists involved in these experiments, was decided upon.
    d. Abundant nitrogens were used by scientists involved in these experiments, which make up about 78 percent of the Earth's atmosphere.

7. Choose the correct way to write the underlined part of sentence 29.

    However, <u>in less time then you can imagine,</u> gasoline-powered vehicles will be things of the past.

    a. in less times then you can imagine,
    b. in less time then you can imagine
    c. in less time than you can imagine,
    d. No change is needed.

8. Choose the **best** way to combine the ideas in sentences 10 and 11 into one sentence.

    Alternative engines power these vehicles. These include electric and fuel-cell-powered types of engines.

    a. Alternative engines, electric, and fuel-cell-powered types of engines, power these vehicles.
    b. Alternative engines power these vehicles, including electric and fuel-cell-powered types of engines.
    c. Alternative engines vehicles, powered by electric engines and fuel-cell-powered engines, power these.
    d. Alternative engines, such as the electric and fuel-cell-powered types, power these vehicles.

9. Which of these is **not** a complete sentence?

    a. One not so dependent upon this non-renewable resource.
    b. The exhaust from the e.Volution's engine will not contain pollutants.
    c. Due to the fact that the e.Volution car runs on air, the company claimed that it caused low levels of pollution or no pollution at all.
    d. It is time to consider a more realistic alternative.

10. Choose the sentence that could **best** be added right after sentence 25.

    a. The Earth's atmosphere is about 21 percent oxygen.
    b. According to the researchers' estimates, a 60-gallon tank will allow the LN2000 to travel about 200 miles.
    c. The e.Volution originated in Europe, whereas this model, the LN2000, is an American-made car.
    d. You should be able to visit your local LN2000 dealership and pick one up today.

George's seventh-grade earth science teacher has asked each student to prepare a report about a location somewhere in the United States where a visitor could see examples of geological wonders. George recently took a trip with his family to New Mexico and toured the Carlsbad Caverns National Park. He wrote his rough draft about what he discovered on his trip. He needs your help editing and revising it.

Here is George's rough draft. Read it and then answer questions 1–10.

(1) While traveling in the Southwestern United States, you may come across a spectacular natural wonder: Carlsbad Caverns National Park. (2) This park is a truley magnificent example of the geological phenomena to be found in our country. (3) It boasts the largest single cavern in the world, the fifth-longest cave network in the world, and the deepest cave in the United States.

(4) The Kings Palace Tour will take you deep and far into the earth. (5) The one-and-a-half-hour ranger-guided tour took you almost a mile underground. (6) A public tour will take you about 830 feet below the surface. (7) You can see columns, soda straws, and draperies. (8) If you decide to make this mighty trek, be sure to be in good health. (9) Children under the age of four are not allowed to make this difficult journey.

(10) The Slaughter Canyon Cave Tour is a two-hour expedition through one and one-fourth miles of underground passageways. (11) There aren't any trails or electricity to guide you on your way a ranger will be there to help you along anyway. (12) All those who go on this Tour will be equipped with a headlamp, however, from the Park Service. (13) This tour boasts some of the most fascinating columns in the world, including the 89-foot-high Monarch Column and the Christmas Tree Column, which is covered in semi-preshus crystals.

(14) An experienced spelunker may want to try either the Spider Cave or Hall of the White Giant Tours. (15) Both last four hours and all participants are expected to be in peak physical condition. (16) You should also not have a fear of tight spaces or heights, as tourists will crawl, climb, and squeeze their way through. (17) This tour is not offered to children less than twelve years of age.

(18) Perhaps the most stunning activity open to visitors to Carlsbad Caverns is the flight of the Mexican free-tailed bats. (19) Each day at sunset in the summer, those bats that dwell in the caverns from April to October will exit the cave in a counterclockwise pattern. (20) In August and September, the event is particularly brilliant, as the young bats join their adult counterparts for the nightly flight.

(21) Of course, not all of Carlsbad Cavern's activities require visitors to hike through underground tunnels. (22) In fact, there are many nature trails that wind their way through the park's outdoor wilderness.

(23) Touring Carlsbad Caverns is not for the timid or for the physically unfit. (24) They recommend that visitors be adequately prepared for all of their adventurous

(continued on next page)

(continued from previous page)

activities. (25) Do not mistakenly believe that the beauty of the landscape makes it any less dangerous. (26) Dress appropriately, bring the right equipment, and have a good understanding of what to expect in this desert area. (27) If you know what to expect and have a taste for great adventure, then Carlsbad Caverns National Park is probably the place for you!

1. Choose the correct way to write the underlined part of sentence 1.

    <u>While traveling in the Southwestern United States,</u> you may come across a spectacular natural wonder: Carlsbad Caverns National Park.

    a. While travelling in the Southwestern United States,
    b. While traveling in the Southwestern united states,
    c. While traveling in the southwestern United States,
    d. No change is needed.

2. George wants to add this sentence to the paragraph that begins with sentence 18.

    They perform the opposite feat at sunrise, returning to the cave before the sun can make its appearance in the sky overhead.

    Where would the sentence **best** fit?

    a. right before sentence 18
    b. right after sentence 18
    c. right after sentence 19
    d. right after sentence 20

3. Read sentence 16, which is poorly written.

    You should also not have a fear of tight spaces or heights, as tourists will crawl, climb, and squeeze their way through.

    Choose the **best** way to rewrite this sentence.

    a. You should also not have a fear of tight spaces, heights should not scare you, as tourists will crawl, climb, and squeeze their way through.
    b. Tourists will crawl, climb, and squeeze their way through, so you should not have a fear of spaces or tight heights.
    c. Tight spaces or heights will scare you if you have a fear of them, so crawl, climb, and squeeze your way past the tourists.
    d. Also, a fear of tight spaces or heights will hinder you, since tourists are expected to crawl, climb, and squeeze their way through these caverns.

216

4. Choose the correct way to write the underlined part of sentence 13.

This tour boasts some of the most fascinating columns in the world, including the 89-foot-high Monarch Column and <u>the Christmas Tree Column, which is covered in semi-preshus crystals.</u>

   a. the Christmas Tree Column, which is, covered in semi-preshus crystals.
   b. the Christmas Tree Column, which is covered in semi-precious crystals.
   c. the christmas tree Column, which is covered in semi-preshus crystals.
   d. No change is needed.

5. Choose the correct way to write the underlined part of sentence 12.

All those who go on <u>this Tour will be equipped with a headlamp, however,</u> from the Park Service.

   a. this tour will be equipped with a headlamp, however,
   b. this Tour will be equiped with a headlamp, however,
   c. this Tour will be equipped with a headlamp however,
   d. No change is needed.

6. Choose the sentence that could **best** be added right after sentence 22.

   a. The Old Guano Road Trail, a 3.7-mile above-ground path through a network of rock cairns, is a popular day hike.
   b. One of these tours boasts the 89-foot-high Monarch Column.
   c. Thank goodness you won't find yourself in the desert in the southwestern United States!
   d. Don't worry about bringing the proper equipment, however, since no visitors are expected to be prepared for the outdoors.

7. Choose the correct way to write the underlined part of sentence 5.

The one-and-a-half-hour <u>ranger-guided tour took you almost</u> a mile underground.

   a. ranger-guided tour takes you almost
   b. ranger-guided, tour took you almost
   c. ranger-guided tour took you allmost
   d. No change is needed.

8. The paragraph that begins with sentence 23 is poorly written. Choose the **best** way to rewrite sentence 27 so that the paragraph does not repeat ideas.

If you know what to expect and have a taste for great adventure, then Carlsbad Caverns National Park is probably the place for you!

a. Carlsbad Caverns National Park is probably the place for you! If you know what to expect and have a taste for adventure.
b. Knowing what to expect and having a taste for adventure are just two reasons to come to Carlsbad Caverns National Park!
c. If you're highly prepared and enthusiastic about outdoor adventures, then Carlsbad Caverns National Park is probably the place for you!
d. Carlsbad Caverns National Park, if you know what to expect and have a taste for great adventure, is the place!

9. Choose the correct way to write the underlined part of sentence 2.

This park is a <u>truley magnificent example of the geological</u> phenomena to be found in our country.

a. truley magnificent example, of the geological
b. truly magnificent example of the geological
c. truley magnificent example of the Geological
d. No change is needed.

10. Read sentence 11, which is poorly written.

There aren't any trails or electricity to guide you on your way a ranger will be there to help you along anyway.

Choose the **best** way to rewrite this sentence.

a. While trails, electricity, and rangers are not there, your way will help you along anyway.
b. Trails and electricity there are not. On your way, a ranger will be there to help you along to guide you.
c. Because trails and electricity are not there to guide the ranger on his or her way, no one is there to help you along.
d. There are neither trails nor electricity to guide you on your way, but a ranger will be there to help you.

Isabella's seventh-grade industrial arts teacher has asked each student to write a report about a new kind of technology he or she hopes to see become part of normal everyday life within the next ten years. Isabella has visited the library, outlined her ideas, and written her rough draft. She needs your help editing and revising it.

Here is Isabella's rough draft. Read it and then answer questions 1–10.

(1) Integrating video game technology into everyday life is one of the most innovative ideas introduced in the past few decades. (2) Augmented reality—the scope of which includes pulling graphics typically only seen on television or computer screens and mingling them with the real world—is by far one of the most advanced and thrilling forms of technology being developed today. (3) Imagine being able to enhance what we see, hear, feel, and smell, all with the cooperation of modern video technology.

(4) The concept of "virtual reality" has been around for quite a while now. (5) This graphic reality creates computer-generated environments and invites people into them, allowing them to nearly become part of a video world. (6) Augmented reality goes a step further by adding graphics to and improving sounds and smells from the real world. (7) Just as many vehicles nowadays have Global Positioning Systems (GPS) to help the driver plot directions and locate him- or herself on a map, people will be able to get computerized information, about where they are and what they are seeing and hearing. (8) Simply by donning a pair of special spectacles, a person will have information right before their very eyes—literally! (9) The enhancements of sound and sight will be refreshed every time the person moves his or her head.

(10) Several high-tech companies and universities are exploring this new medium. (11) They hope to perfecting the means by which people can enhance what they are having experienced in their environment. (12) As with all scientific discoveries, however, mistakes must be made in order to obtain the desired result.

(13) A head-mounted display (HMD) resembles a pair of skiing goggles. (14) It will allow people to see graphics and text much like a computer monitor. (15) Video see-through displays block out the wearer's surroundings. (16) They use tiny video cameras to capture images of the environment. (17) Like looking through the lens of a camera. (18) The person sees a video image of the real environment with graphics laid over that video. (19) Video see-through displays have one major problem: to much time lapses between what the cameras capture and what they project to the person wearing the headset.

(20) Tracking systems for augmented reality must be even accurater than those systems currently in use, such as GPS. (21) GPS can be as much as ten to thirty meters off its target. (22) A person using a similar device needs more precision than that. (23) An augmented reality system that projects images at a distance of twenty meters ahead would be worthless to the person wearing it. (24) Therefore, the tracking system must still be refined in order for augmented reality to become part of our everyday lives.

(continued on next page)

(continued from previous page)

(25) Technology has come far since Pong was first introduced to video arcades in the 1970s. (26) Every year, we see video game graphics becoming smoother and more advanced. (27) Practical three-dimensional systems like augmented reality would improve our lives considerably by making our knowledge of the world around we even clearer. (28) At the rate we're going now, within just a few years men and women from all walks of life can experience augmented reality.

1. Choose the correct way to write the underlined part of sentence 8.

   Simply by donning a pair of special spectacles, a person will have information right <u>before their very eyes—literally!</u>

   a. before their very eyes: literally!
   b. before their very eyes—literally?
   c. before his or her very eyes—literally!
   d. No change is needed.

2. Isabella wants to add this sentence to the paragraph that begins with sentence 10.

   So far, however, the prototypes have been somewhat bulky and imperfect.

   Where would the sentence **best** fit?

   a. right before sentence 10
   b. right after sentence 10
   c. right after sentence 11
   d. right after sentence 12

3. Choose the correct way to write the underlined part of sentence 19.

   Video see-through displays have one major problem: <u>to much time lapses between what the cameras</u> capture and what they project to the person wearing the headset.

   a. too much time lapses between what the cameras
   b. to much time lapses between what the camera's
   c. to much time lapsed between what the cameras
   d. No change is needed.

220

4. Which of these is **not** a complete sentence?

   a. Imagine being able to enhance what we see, hear, feel, and smell, all with the cooperation of modern video technology.
   b. The concept of "virtual reality" has been around for quite a while now.
   c. Like looking through the lens of a camera.
   d. At the rate we're going now, within just a few years men and women from all walks of life can experience augmented reality.

5. Choose the correct way to write the underlined part of sentence 20.

   Tracking systems for augmented reality <u>must be even accurater than</u> those systems currently in use, such as GPS.

   a. must be even more accurate than
   b. must be even accurater then
   c. must been even accurater than
   d. No change is needed.

6. Choose the **best** way to combine the ideas in sentences 21 and 22 into one sentence.

   GPS can be as much as ten to thirty meters off its target. A person using a similar device needs more precision than that.

   a. GPS can be as much as ten to thirty meters off its target, so a person using a similar device needs more precision than that.
   b. GPS can be as much as ten to thirty meters off its target, but a person needs a more precise device to rely upon.
   c. A person using a similar device, like GPS, needs more precision than that.
   d. As much as ten to thirty meters off its target, GPS is a much more precise device for people to use.

7. Choose the correct way to write the underlined part of sentence 7.

Just as many vehicles nowadays have Global Positioning Systems (GPS) to help the driver plot directions and locate him- or herself on a map, people will be able to get <u>computerized information, about where they are and what they are seeing and hearing.</u>

   a. computerized information, about where they are and what there seeing and hearing.
   b. computerized information about where they are and what they are seeing and hearing.
   c. computerized information, about where they are and what they are see and hear.
   d. No change is needed.

8. Read sentence 11, which is poorly written.

They hope to perfecting the means by which people can enhance what they are having experienced in their environment.

Choose the **best** way to rewrite this sentence.

   a. They hope that people can enhance what they are having experienced in their environment.
   b. In their environment, they hope to perfecting the way by which people can enhance their environment.
   c. By experiencing their environment enhanced, they hope to perfect the means by which people can enhance what they are having.
   d. They hope to perfect the means by which people can enhance they are experiencing in their environment.

9. Choose the correct way to write the underlined part of sentence 27.

Practical three-dimensional systems like augmented reality would improve our lives considerably by making our knowledge <u>of the world around we even clearer.</u>

a. of the world around we even more clear.
b. of the world around we even clearer?
c. of the world around us even clearer.
d. No change is needed.

10. Read sentence 5, which is poorly written.

This graphic reality creates computer-generated environments and invites people into them, allowing them to nearly become part of a video world.

Choose the **best** way to rewrite this sentence.

a. This graphic reality creates computer-generated environments. Invites people into them. Allowing them to nearly become part of a video world.
b. By allowing them to nearly become part of a video world, this graphic reality creates computer-generated environments.
c. This graphic reality, which creates computer-generated environments, invites people to almost become part of a video world.
d. Creates computer-generated environments and this graphic reality invites people into them by allowing them to almost become part of a video world.

Denver's history class has been studying Nostradamus, a man born in the sixteenth century whose predictions for the future of humankind have astounded historians and scientists alike for centuries. His teacher has asked each student to explain how Nostradamus was able to make predictions about a time so vastly different and distant from his own. Denver has devised his own set of ideas and written his rough draft. He needs your help editing and revising it.

Here is Denver's rough draft. Read it and then answer questions 1–10.

(1) Consider the following true story: In 1898, Morgan Robertson published a novel, *Futility*, in which a luxery liner called the *Titan* crashes into an iceberg one April night while traveling through dense fog. (2) In the story, the ship sinks and hundreds of people die. (3) Robertson claimed that the story came to him while he was in a trance. (4) Fourteen years following the book's publication, the *Titanic* fell to an identical fate, which was similar in size and structure to the *Titan*. (5) Even the reason for high casualty numbers—too few lifeboats on board—was the same in both accounts. (6) Could Robertson have been unknowingly foretelling the future? (7) Was it an extrasensory experience or merely coinsidense?

(8) People often claim that they have the ability to see into the future. (9) In fact, some people make a living off that claim. (10) Is it truly possible to foretell what is going to happen tomorrow or fifty years from now? (11) Do certain people possess a sixth sense called "extrasensory perception" (ESP,) which some believe to be beyond sight, hearing, smell, touch, and taste? (12) Many people are convinced that we all have the ability to experience our world both physically and on some higher astral plane. (13) Others feel that only certain people can channel and harness this powerful energy. (14) The common belief among those who put faith in ESP is that some people are more attuned to their perceptions than others.

(15) By the common definition, ESP is not a bodily sense. (16) Rather than being a physical response to something in the environment, ESP typically manifests itself in thoughts. (17) There are several different kinds of ESP. (18) Telepathy is the ability to read someone else's thoughts. (19) Clairvoyance is the ability to see something occurring in another place. (20) Precognition is the ability to see into the future.

(21) The idea that people could perceive things outside of their bodily senses is not a new one. (22) However, ESP as we understand it does not develop until the twentieth century. (23) Duke University professor J.B. Rhine coined the term "ESP" in 1934. (24) Rhine was one of the first respected scientists to research and test paranormal phenomena in a university laboratory.

(25) Since it is exceedingly difficult to scientifically prove the existence of ESP, there are many conflicting theories regarding how it works. (26) Like religious concepts, ESP does not fit into a scientific model. (27) In fact, it similarly depends on the existence

(continued on next page)

224

(continued from previous page)

of a soul dwelling in a reality outside of the bounds of our physical laws. (28) Some people purport that ESP is a result of something coming from a place beyond the known physical world. (29) As time and space work differently in this parallel reality, believers claim that people are allowed to easily flow in and out of other's thoughts and sometimes can see the distant past and future. (30) Our conscious mind may often be unaware of this other plane, but phenomena will manifest still themselves from time to time.

(31) So was Robertson truly able to foretell the *Titanic* tragedy? (32) Are the predictions of Nostradamus mere coincidences? (33) Or is it comforting for some people to believe that we have a higher awareness of the world around us? (34) It is hard to know for sure.

1. Choose the correct way to write the underlined part of sentence 29.

    As time and space work differently in this parallel reality, believers claim that people are allowed to <u>easily flow in and out of other's thoughts</u> and sometimes can see the distant past and future.

    a. more easy flow in and out of other's thoughts
    b. easily flow in and out of others' thoughts
    c. easily flow in and out of other's thought's
    d. No change is needed.

2. Choose the correct way to write the underlined part of sentence 1.

    Consider the following true story: In 1898, Morgan Robertson published a novel, *Futility*, in which <u>a luxery liner called the *Titan* crashes</u> into an iceberg one April night while traveling through dense fog.

    a. a luxury liner called the *Titan* crashes
    b. a luxery liner called, the *Titan*, crashes
    c. a luxery liner call the *Titan* crashes
    d. No change is needed.

3. Choose the correct way to write the underlined part of sentence 31.

    So was Robertson truly able to <u>foretell the *Titanic* tragedy?</u>

    a. foretell the *Titanic* tragedy!
    b. fourtell the *Titanic* tragedy?
    c. foretell the *titanic* tragedy?
    d. No change is needed.

4. Choose the sentence that could **best** be added right after sentence 34.

    a. The best part of being an American is having the freedom to speak your mind.
    b. If you want to be a scientist, then I wouldn't suggest believing in ESP.
    c. Fortunately, it is the existence of mysteries such as this that make life more interesting.
    d. Whenever you come upon someone who appears to be a bit odd, you can safely assume that they are tapping into their subconscious mind.

5. Choose the correct way to write the underlined part of sentence 11.

Do certain people possess a sixth sense <u>called "extrasensory perception" (ESP,) which</u> some believe to be beyond sight, hearing, smell, touch, and taste?

    a. calls "extrasensory perception" (ESP,) which
    b. called, "extrasensory perception" (ESP,) which
    c. called "extrasensory perception" (ESP), which
    d. No change is needed.

6. Choose the word or phrase that **best** fits at the beginning of sentence 5.

    a. However,
    b. Nevertheless,
    c. As a result,
    d. In fact,

7. Choose the correct way to write the underlined part of sentence 22.

However, ESP as we understand it <u>does not develop until the twentieth century.</u>

    a. did not develop until the twentieth century.
    b. does not develop until the Twentieth Century.
    c. does not develop until, the twentieth century.
    d. No change is needed.

8. Choose the correct way to write the underlined part of sentence 7.

Was it an <u>extrasensory experience or merely coinsidense?</u>

   a. extrasensory experience or merely coincidence?
   b. extrasensory experience or merely coinsidense.
   c. extrasensory, experience or merely coinsidense?
   d. No change is needed.

9. Denver wants to change sentence 13 so that it is more specific.

Others feel that only certain <u>people can channel and harness this powerful energy.</u>

Choose the **best** way to rewrite the underlined part of this sentence.

   a. people can channel and harness this powerful energy, while some can't.
   b. people, such as psychics, shamans, or mediums, can channel and harness this powerful energy.
   c. people may or may not know if they can channel and harness this powerful energy.
   d. powerful energy can be channeled or harnessed by people.

10. Read sentence 4, which is poorly written.

Fourteen years following the book's publication, the *Titanic* fell to an identical fate, which was similar in size and structure to the *Titan*.

Choose the **best** way to rewrite this sentence.

   a. After fourteen years, the book's publication about the *Titanic* showed a similarity between the fictional ship and its real-life size and structure, the *Titan*.
   b. The *Titanic* fell to an identical fate, which was similar in size and structure to the *Titan* fourteen years later.
   c. The book was published, the *Titanic* fell to an identical fate, the size and structure was similar, and the *Titan* came fourteen years earlier.
   d. Fourteen years following the book's publication, the *Titanic*, which was similar in size and structure to the *Titan*, fell to an identical fate.

Made in United States
North Haven, CT
15 February 2024

48767184R00128